Praise for *Evolving E*

"*Evolving Education* is an inspirational a
to a learner-centered approach. It clear
success, create powerful learning experiences, and support them with enabling conditions. *Evolving Education* would make a great book study for any school faculty or community group."

—**Tom Vander Ark,** CEO of *Getting Smart*, author, and international thought leader

"Katie Martin absolutely nailed it in *Evolving Education*. The book continually challenges us to ask ourselves, 'What does it mean to be successful?' and 'How can we design classrooms, schools, and systems to improve the lives of the students we serve?' A learner-centered paradigm requires that we examine beliefs and biases and disrupt systems that do not serve each and every learner. This work requires innovation, creativity, flexibility, and heart. This book is the perfect mix of incredible storytelling, inspiration, and concrete strategy."

—**Katie Novak, EdD,** educational consultant and author of nine books, including *UDL and Blended Learning*

"Dewey, Marzano, and Hattie delivered a modern pedagogy connected to tangible practices and authentic examples from the field; Katie Martin provides the next chapter. *Evolving Education* will be relevant for decades to come. If there's one book to put in the hands of teachers and school leaders to help make the shift to learner-centered classrooms and schools, it is this one."

—**David Miyashiro, EdD,** superintendent of Cajon Valley Union School District

"Thought-provoking and inspiring! Shifting the narrative from deficit-thinking to an asset-based approach, this book empowers educators with the mindset and practices needed to evolve. Dr. Martin weaves together stories and research to illustrate the power of a culture of care and agency that maximizes the curiosity, passions, and talents of all learners. If you are ready to evolve beyond a compliance-driven model and innovate to authentic, learner-centered education, this book is a must-read!"

—**Lainie Rowell,** lead author of *Evolving Learner* and international education consultant

"Filled with Katie's personal experiences, her extensive research and practice, and authentic educator stories, *Evolving Education* is a book that will inspire educators to more closely connect with learners and create experiences to help them thrive! *Evolving Education* is a must-read for anyone in education looking to improve their teaching practice and expand the types of learning experiences they provide for all students."

—**Rachelle Dene Poth,** ISTE-certified educator, teacher, consultant, speaker, attorney, author, and blogger

"Katie Martin does it again! This is an incredible book by a brilliant thinker who has skillfully connected personal stories, research, and professional insights from working with hundreds of schools into frameworks and practical suggestions to inspire and guide the shift to learner-centered education. *Evolving Education* is an instant classic, and it is essential reading to inform effective and empowered learning for all."

—**Devin Vodicka, EdD,** chief impact officer of Learner-Centered Collaborative and the author of *Learner-Centered Leadership*

"If we are going to address systemic inequity in our schools, then we need to take an approach that is focused on the diverse needs of our students and less on the perceived needs of the school. This approach requires identifying the skills that all students must develop. Katie Martin shows us that these skills are not just an add-on to our school curriculum but the foundation to learning in our schools. Dr. Martin's learner-centered paradigm shows us the way to move our schools forward. For those of us who care deeply about equity, our students need to be the center of our approach. Katie Martin not only shows us how to do this, but how to do it well.

Now is the time to move the needs of every student into the center of our schools, and now is the time for this book."

—**Henry Turner, EdD,** high school principal, speaker, and writer

"*Evolving Education* issues the bold challenge for educators to consider it an obligation to create the conditions for students to be at the center of learning. The timing is right for practices to shift, and this book fuels the inspiration to take action. *Evolving Education* is more than a must-read; it offers a number of must-apply practices for all readers."

—**Marlon Styles,** superintendent of Middletown Public Schools

"Katie Martin is one of my favorite educational authors because she has a wonderful ability to combine the big picture with specific illustrations and practical strategies. In her new book, Martin thoughtfully weaves together important ideas, inspiring stories about learning, and concrete examples from schools to help us understand the large and small shifts that are necessary for an 'evolving education.' Each chapter includes numerous scenarios, provocations, and guiding questions that will get you thinking deeply, and there is an emphasis throughout the book on creating systems, not just isolated pockets of innovation. If you care about transforming student learning, *Evolving Education* should be a keystone book in your school-improvement library."

—**Dr. Scott McLeod,** professor at University of Colorado Denver and founding director of CASTL

"In *Evolving Education*, Dr. Katie Martin provides a much-needed inspirational resource for how every educator can transform their classroom and culture into an environment that prioritizes the needs, curiosity, and futures of young people. From provocations that help educators reflect on their practices to strategies that support schools designing personalized pathways for learning, this book shows us how to create engaging, learner-centered spaces. With stories from her own life and examples of pedagogical practices like project-based learning and design thinking as well as the current research on the science of learning, Dr. Martin illustrates why we need to change education and also how to do it. Perhaps most importantly, Dr. Martin takes a deep look at the process of change—addressing the emotional arc of transforming one's practice and acknowledging that as we change our teaching practices and shift the culture of schools, we too are transformed into the educators our students need us to be."

—**Laura McBain,** K12 lab director of community and implementation at Stanford d.school

Evolving Education

EVOLVING EDUCATION

SHIFTING TO A LEARNER-CENTERED PARADIGM

Dr. Katie Martin

Evolving Education: Shifting to a Learner-Centered Paradigm

Published by IMPress, a division of Dave Burgess Consulting, Inc.
IMPressbooks.org
DaveBurgessConsulting.com
San Diego, CA

Library of Congress Control Number: 2021941525
Paperback ISBN: 978-1-948334-34-1
Ebook ISBN: 978-1-948334-35-8

Cover design by Emily Mahon
Interior design by Liz Schreiter
Editing and production by Reading List Editorial: readinglisteditorial.com

To my husband, Matt:
You have believed in me from day one and have given me the courage and support to pursue my passions. You are, by far, my favorite teacher, and I couldn't ask for a better partner to navigate life with. I love you.

CONTENTS

INTRODUCTION

FROM SCHOOL-CENTERED TO LEARNER-CENTERED

The year 2020 was a whirlwind. Seemingly overnight, educators had to shift from in-person to remote teaching, leaving well-established resources, tools, and procedures behind. It felt as if the ground was being pulled out from under us. Gone was the schedule that kept us all in place, guiding our curriculum as we moved reliably from class to class, from year to year. Gone was the security in a predictable system that allowed us to feel safe going through the motions. Many of us rarely questioned this process because the structures that kept the system in place looked more or less the same for a hundred years.

But sometimes a shock to the system is exactly what it takes to bring about much-needed change. As the Irish poet Oscar Wilde once wrote, "Without structure, nothing can exist. Without chaos, nothing can evolve."[1] The chaos of 2020 and the beginning of 2021 forced us to come up with new strategies and models to educate our students. It was not easy, and it will have a lasting impact on every aspect of our lives, but if we are open to it, there are lessons to be gleaned. There is an opportunity to rethink our practices, intentionally leave behind those that don't best serve all learners and educators, and be more intentional about incorporating what matters most: relationships, connection, purpose, flexibility, agency, and authentic learning. The pandemic created an opening for us to free ourselves of preexisting norms and expectations and enter the realm of possibility.

I want to be clear: This is not a book about the great pandemic and the chaos of the 2020–2021 school year. This is a book about expanding our mental models of what is possible so we can best meet the needs of all learners—anytime, anywhere. In my previous book, *Learner-Centered Innovation*, I focused on a greater vision for an education system and how professional learning could support key shifts for educators. Consequently, this book offers a deeper dive into how we can harness new technologies, learning sciences, and pedagogy that center learners and learning. We'll explore practical tools for creating a learner-centered, network-age model of education characterized by connection, flexibility, agency, and contribution. My hope is to share learner-centered practices that both validate and push your thinking, inspire you with ideas and examples, and fuel your purpose and passion to create learning experiences that truly enable all children to reach their full potential.

From School-Centered to Learner-Centered

When we look to learners, we can see what's working and what's challenging, and ultimately, we can start to envision what's possible. Evolution in education is about using insight from our own experiences, research from the field, and new tools and approaches to adapt our practice to best meet learners where they are. I have two children, Abby and Zack, who are both unique individuals with their own strengths, challenges, and goals. What matters most to me as a mom is that my children know that they matter for who they are and who they are becoming. I want them to know how to learn when no one is telling them what to do, how to fight for something that matters to them, how to communicate their ideas, feelings, and dreams. I want them to have the skills to work with others in diverse and complex situations to solve problems that matter to them and others. I want this for *all* of us. And that's where learner-centered education comes in.

Learner-centered education puts learners at the center of their own education in order to create more purposeful, personalized, authentic, and competency-based experiences that help them develop skills that empower them to learn, grow, and solve problems that matter to them and others. It's a paradigm shift that changes how we *see* learners and how we assess which learning experiences are most effective for each individual. This shift begins with an awareness that if we truly want to develop knowledge, habits, and skills in students, we have to know them, love them, and help them see the full beauty of who they are and what they can become.

Some people may read the above and think, *Well, we can't just let students do whatever they want. What about the basics?* I believe the dichotomy between learner-centered practices and the "basics" is a false tension. In a learner-centered ecosystem, the basics are critical to developing expertise, and students need instruction, practice, and feedback as they develop these foundational skills. At the same time, when these skills are necessary for learners to solve meaningful problems in a relevant context and are purposeful for them, students become much more motivated to learn and integrate these skills now and in their future.

When students struggle to acquire necessary skills, a learner-centered approach asks us to reframe the way we look at the problem. What if creating rigid structures and standardized learning experiences doesn't allow for students to develop the skills and practice necessary to solve problems, communicate, and collaborate effectively? What if students who aren't seen for their unique gifts and talents, who don't have opportunities to participate in fun and meaningful school experiences, are the ones who become disengaged? What if the ways we have traditionally expected students to learn in school is fundamentally misaligned with what we actually know about *how* we learn?

Shifting to a learner-centered paradigm is not just about adding more. Fundamentally, it is about changing our way of thinking about and how we see learners and what is possible in education. The following chart, adapted from Education Reimagined's report "A Transformational Vison for the US," breaks down the basic components of a shift from school- to learner-centered education that each chapter will focus on.[2]

From School-Centered	To Learner-Centered
Teach to the average and manage expectations.	Variability is the norm, and the uniqueness of learners is something to build upon.
Relationships and SEL are secondary to learning.	Relationships and SEL are the foundation of effective learning communities.
Learners are sorted and ranked.	Everyone is capable of learning and contributing in meaningful ways.
Success is defined by GPAs and standardized test scores.	Success is defined on an individual basis; each learner has their own unique strengths, interests, and goals.
Focus on the most effective teaching.	Focus on producing the most effective learning.
Learners follow a standardized path, place, and pace to assess proficiency.	Learners move at their pace and follow the path that allows them to demonstrate a mastery of knowledge, skills, and dispositions.
Learners adapt to the standardized system.	The system adapts to meet the needs of the learner.
Learners must be compelled to learn.	Learners want to learn.
Education is done to the learner.	Education is done by (and with) the learner.

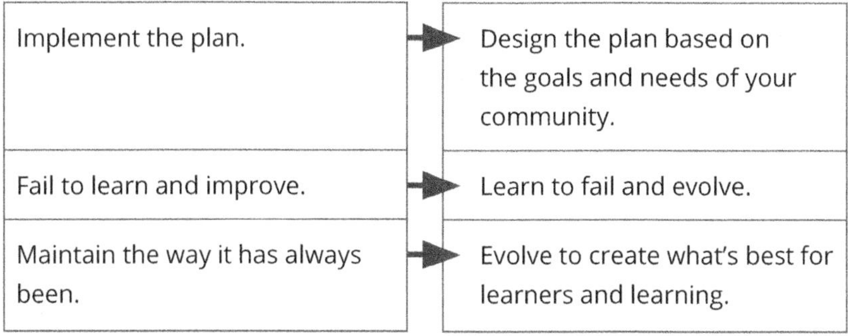

Implement the plan.	Design the plan based on the goals and needs of your community.
Fail to learn and improve.	Learn to fail and evolve.
Maintain the way it has always been.	Evolve to create what's best for learners and learning.

To address these shifts, this book is broken into three essential questions:

PART I: WHAT ARE OUR ASPIRATIONS FOR LEARNERS? I share an overview of what it means to start with a holistic understanding of each learner as an individual rather than emphasizing averages and standardization. We'll look at what it means to get to know each learner and treat each one as if they are capable of learning and contributing in their own, meaningful way. And we'll explore what it might look like to redefine success and expand measure beyond GPAs, standardized tests, and traditional methods of assessment.

PART II: HOW MIGHT WE CREATE THE MOST IMPACTFUL LEARNING EXPERIENCES? In this section, we'll explore key elements of learner-centered education: the art and science of learning, competency-based learning, personalized learning, empowered learning, and authentic learning. We'll look at real-world examples that I hope will validate you, push you, and inspire you to take action. It's not about changing everything; it's often the smallest shifts that can ignite change and lead to a great impact.

PART III: HOW MIGHT WE CREATE THE ENABLING CONDITIONS TO SHIFT TO A LEARNER-CENTERED PARADIGM? While the first section will delve into how we see learners, and the second will focus on the key practices, the final section will zone in on how we can shift our mindset. We will look to human-centered design to consider the ways we might bring about more widespread, systemic change. We will explore examples and practical tips to challenge the status quo and create the experiences our students deserve.

This following graphic represents each section of the book, and you will see it at the beginning of each section. I often refer to this as the learner-centered ecosystem, represented in three concentric circles. They all are interdependent, but we start at the center with learners and the desired outcomes, then design the learning experiences that align to our desired outcomes, and finally, ensure the enabling conditions are in place to support what we want for learners.

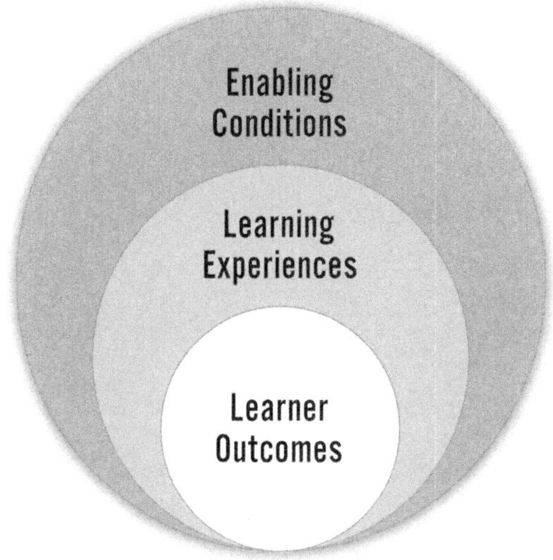

From Beliefs to Practice

In *Learner-Centered Innovation*, I challenged educators to ask themselves the following questions:

- Am I improving students' lives?
- Am I working to make the world a better place by creating more thoughtful, compassionate, creative, and skilled individuals?
- Am I providing opportunities for individuals to contribute positively to the local and global communities with which they interact?

I still believe these are the right questions for teachers to ask themselves, but I also know working on our beliefs and aspirations is only the first step. Truly evolving education requires each and every teacher to take concrete action. This book will offer you examples, strategies, and frameworks to help you evolve in your practice.

Along the journey, I will share insights as a mom, an educator, and a learner. I am also the daughter and wife of amazing teachers. I see the world through all of these lenses, so you will read stories about my family in the coming pages, especially my children, Abby and Zack. You will learn about the educators and students I have met as I walked the halls and visited thousands of classrooms all over the world. I have been in schools with high poverty rates and extreme wealth, from urban to rural, and although each context varies, the potential that exists in each of the students and communities does not. In each context, I've encountered amazing educators who are meeting their students where they are and creating learner-centered experiences that expand opportunities for their futures.

A fundamental shift in education is within reach. In fact, it's already happening all around us, possibly in your own teaching practice. As you read, I hope you feel validated and can celebrate what you've already done to positively impact those you serve. I also want to push your thinking about what's possible, address the barriers (perceived and real) that hold you back, and inspire you to learn, fail, and pick yourself and others back up as you work together to make amazing things happen for young people and for us as educators. Each chapter has questions at the end for you to jot down your ideas and "Put It into Practice," then share them with your team or with all of us using #EvolvingEducation to expand your community and impact. I can't wait to learn with you and see the learner-centered experiences you create.

Let's get started!

PART I

WHAT ARE OUR ASPIRATIONS FOR LEARNERS?

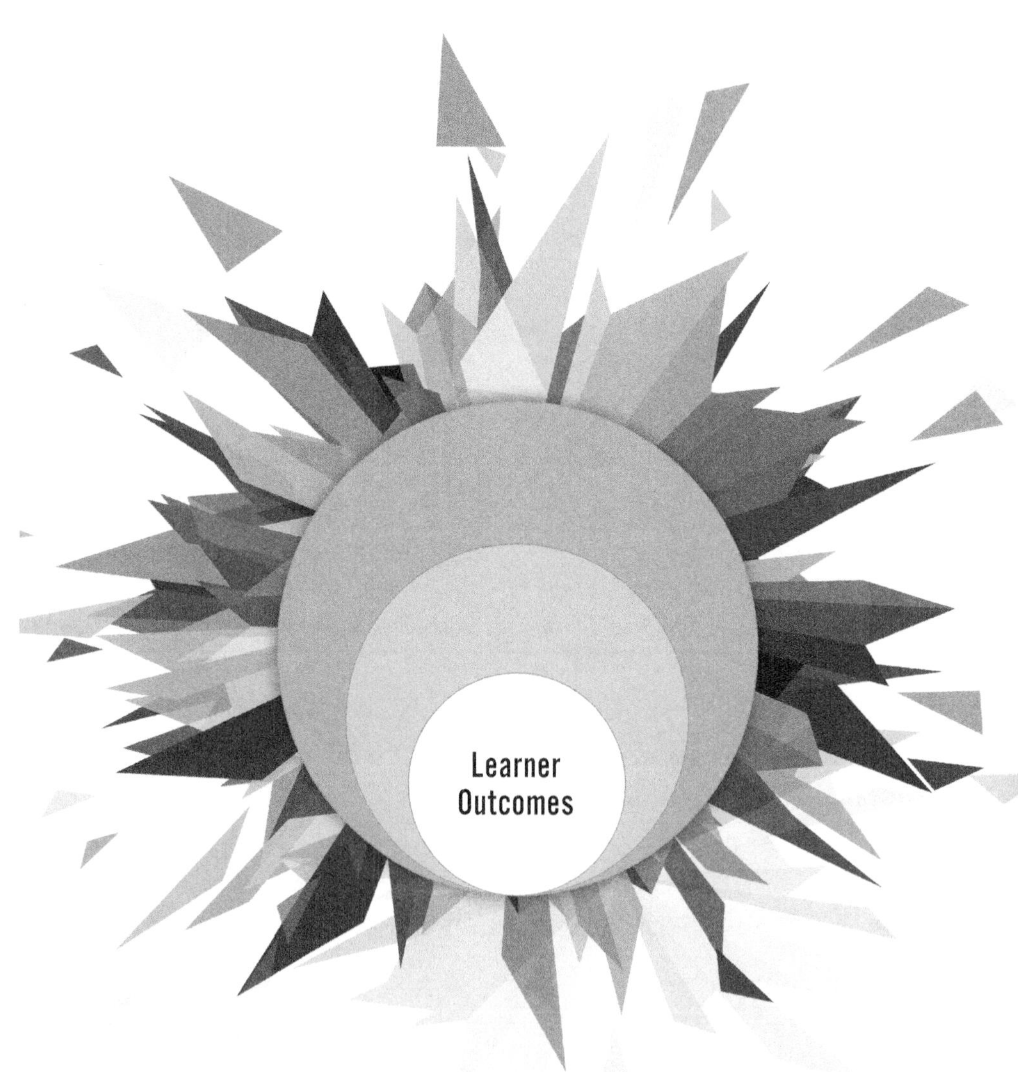

In part I, we will start with why it matters to create a holistic understanding of each learner as an individual rather than emphasizing averages and standardization. We'll look at how to get to know each learner and what's possible when you believe each learner is capable of learning and contributing in their own meaningful way. And we'll explore what it might look like to redefine success and expand measure beyond GPAs, standardized tests, and traditional methods of assessment.

Through chapters 1 to 4, these key shifts will be addressed.

From School-Centered		To Learner-Centered
Teach to the average and manage expectations.	→	Variability is the norm, and the uniqueness of learners is something to build upon.
Relationships and SEL are secondary to learning.	→	Relationships and SEL are the foundation of effective learning communities.
Learners are sorted and ranked.	→	Everyone is capable of learning and contributing in meaningful ways.
Success is defined by GPAs and standardized test scores.	→	Success is defined on an individual basis; each learner has their own unique strengths, interests, and goals.

KNOW YOUR LEARNERS (AND HELP THEM KNOW THEMSELVES)

Teach to the average and manage expectations.	→	*Variability is the norm, and the uniqueness of learners is something to build upon.*

Zack is my youngest and has always been a very sweet and caring boy. He is known to be a great friend, one who always makes sure the new kids in class are included and one who loves when everyone can play and get along together. He loves playing sports and winning, and most importantly, his coaches have always commended him on his "coachability" and sportsmanship, which makes us so proud. He leaves me sweet notes or sends me his favorite GIFs when I travel. Zack recently made the leap from binge-reading *Captain Underpants* to devouring the *Harry Potter* series and determining that he is a Hufflepuff, whose characteristics include a strong sense of justice, loyalty, patience, and a propensity for hard work.

Zack also loves to solve puzzles and has an incredible knack for numbers. He has always been a builder and loves his LEGO sets. He can sit for extended periods of time with an intense focus on puzzles, projects he values, or Minecraft world-creating. His independence and confidence in his creations is a beautiful thing.

I am sharing this because, like all parents, I think the world of my son, but also because I want you to have the context of who my son is and how I see him before I share how he was seen in school. This is his midyear progress report from second grade.

ENGLISH LANGUAGE ARTS			
Reading: Reads a range of increasingly complex literary and informational texts to construct and convey meaning	2	2	
Writing: Conveys information and ideas in writing for a range of purposes and audiences	2	2	
Speaking and Listening: Employs effective speaking and listening skills for a range of purposes and audiences	3	2	
Language: Demonstrates command of academic language and the conventions of English when reading, writing, and speaking	2	1	
Foundational Skills: Applies grade-appropriate word analysis skills to support accurate and fluent reading	2	2	

Although Zack is funny, curious, and caring, among so many other things, he wasn't always recognized for those traits in school. What was measured and valued didn't create a holistic account of his strengths and challenges. He had mostly twos (out of four) on his report card in the first marking period, and what is even worse is that we saw his scores decline during the second marking period.

When I looked at a sample of his work, I could certainly make the argument that his work clearly earned those ones and twos. He often wrote one-word answers, and his penmanship was hard to read. The grading and lack of meaningful feedback in the form of a few question marks he received from his teacher confirmed that this type of schooling was certainly not working. And Zack was miserable. He painfully pointed out that although I was working so hard to fix schools, it wasn't working. He looked at me pleadingly and asked, "How much longer do I have to do this, Mom?" #MomFail

Zack was in a school that was rated very high on conventional metrics based on their exceptional test scores. I also knew his teacher cared about him and all her students. She was working very hard in a system that was designed for an industrial era. The result was often standardization, compliance, isolated content, and the completion of tasks. Like all systems, it was perfectly designed to get the results it got.

What the late Sir Ken Robinson helped me and the world understand through his powerful TED talk "Do Schools Kill Creativity?" is that "one of the roles of education is to awaken and develop the powers of creativity. Instead, what we have is a culture of standardization."[1] It is increasingly clear that we need to honor and develop students' abilities to think differently, solve problems, and navigate new and different situations. We also need to teach and support the development of skills that enable students to develop their own path along with social and emotional intelligence so they can thrive in a constantly changing and unpredictable society. This means we can't structure the learning experiences with a fixed curriculum that is outdated or fails to reflect the complexity of diverse perspectives. We can't be satisfied with merely covering content or meeting standards. Endless possibilities exist to structure learning experiences for students to discover problems to solve, ideas to develop, and feedback to receive on the value of their ideas and products.

A Learner-Centered Environment

Fast-forward to the following school year. Zack came home in the first few weeks and said, "Mom, did you know I'm smart?" I said, "Of course I do, buddy, but what made you realize it?"

He explained, "Miss Hassey gave us a really hard math problem and we all used our own strategies to figure it out. She picked mine to share with the class!" It was a simple and powerful strategy that began to shift his mindset. This validation and encouragement that he had value and could solve problems in ways that made sense to him instead of just completing a worksheet was one of many breakthroughs he experienced as a result of a caring educator who intentionally created a learner-centered environment. His teacher was focused on developing the knowledge, skills, and mindsets of learners and, in doing so, created an equitable learning community that prioritized personalization, learner agency, authentic work, and meaningful contribution.

We saw just how impactful this approach was for Zack during parent-teacher-conference week. Miss Hassey started the conference by providing time for each of us to highlight something we were proud of Zack for. This alone was powerful and gave us an opportunity to celebrate the strengths my son has. Then, Zack led the conference by sharing how he was doing overall in school based on the goals he had discussed with his teacher and classmates, how he was doing socially, and some of his goals in both areas. He then showed us some strategies he had been learning in math and discussed what he was reading and the challenge of finding anything that could compare to *Harry Potter*. The struggle was real! As he opened his notebook and shared what he had been writing, I could see he was so proud of his work. He looked at us, and I looked at the full pages he had filled. His teacher looked at us, and Zack read his favorite reading response, which he had preselected. As Miss Hassey shared how she had seen Zack improve so much over the past year in his writing, especially with his organization and effort, I could barely keep it together. In fact, I am sitting here in tears as I write this.

We all celebrated his unique gifts, then he proceeded to present a slideshow he had prepared. He talked about how he had grown as a writer, reader, and mathematician. With each slide, he shared the skills he'd learned and his strengths, challenges, and goals. He was articulate, proud, and honest about his next steps as a learner. It was a dramatic shift in his confidence and competence.

After Zack presented his work to us, Miss Hassey shared her assessment of where he was in regard to academic norms on reading, writing, and math, what standards he had mastered, and what he still needed to work on. More importantly, she shared, "Zack is a wonderful friend. He jumped right into his new class and has flourished. Zack understands the importance of making others feel included, has a healthy, diverse range of friends, and is considered a good friend by many. Zack's positive and welcoming spirit is impressive for his age." In that moment, it was so clear why Zack was flourishing: he had a teacher and a community who saw him for his many gifts, just as we got to see outside of school. To be fair, she also acknowledged his areas for growth. "Zack is working on compromising and problem-solving by meeting in the middle of multiple people's points of view." Yup. She really got him.

I barely held back my tears when I asked him what had changed to make such a dramatic improvement in his writing. He said, "I decided that I really wanted people to be able to read and understand my ideas, so I slowed down and have been trying much harder to organize my ideas." All attempts to keep it together were a lost cause, and through tears, all I could say was, "I am so proud of you!" but I was feeling so much more—relieved, hopeful, inspired, and so grateful for his amazing teacher who made the choice to focus on learners and learning first then design her systems, policies, and learning experiences to meet students where they were and foster the unique and special individuals they were becoming.

Every time I tell Zack's story, people come up to me and say they know someone—maybe even their own child—who has experienced the same thing. This is because the system was designed for standardization. Even though many educators and other highly successful people will say the system worked for them, the reality is we have too many learners who don't feel seen or valued. Too often, these students and families have suffered in silence or without options, thinking there was something wrong with them instead of something wrong with the system. We can and should have many modes to meet learners where they are. We don't need young people to adapt to a standardized system; we need the system to adapt to the unique learners.

Building on the Strengths, Interests, and Goals of Each Learner

Rather than approach learners with a deficit-based lens, we can work to understand and build on their unique strengths and talents to help them develop the skills, knowledge, and mindsets they need to see their full potential. Implementing graduate profiles, profiles of success, or learner profiles is increasingly popular, as these models can help expand the collective idea of success, foster foundational knowledge and content, and elevate the essential knowledge, skills, and mindsets learners need to thrive now and in their future.

I am all for this and believe it is a critical step, but I also know that it has to move beyond posters and the strategic plan to truly make an impact on learners and their learning. Too often, the learner profile acknowledges the skills we value, but when it comes to report cards, only the academics standards are assessed, measured, and shared. When we set goals, capture evidence, and share what students are doing in connection with our learner profile, we expand the view of success and help students develop the skills to get there.

Make the Knowledge, Skills, and Habits That are Valued in Your Community Explicitly Clear and Accessible to Students

The words in the learner profile matter, but defining them and showing examples is a critical step in making them accessible and creating a shared understanding of the goal. I like the way Oak Knoll Elementary School in Northern California created indicators to help make this clearer.[2]

Exemplary Scholar	Valued Friend	Courageous Citizens
Critical Thinking **I can solve complex problems.** ❑ Ask on topic questions to understand problems ❑ Seek and consider different perspectives ❑ Judge the credibility of sources ❑ Notice and explain different solutions ❑ Apply thinking skills to new and challenging tasks	**Self-Reflection** **I know myself.** ❑ Identify and communicate emotions ❑ Use strategies to work through challenging emotions ❑ Identify strengths, interests, and areas of growth and then build from them ❑ Know family history, culture, and various personal identities ❑ Understand and explain their impact on others	**Agency** **My voice matters.** ❑ Share ideas and opinions with others ❑ Speak up for myself and others, even when it's hard ❑ Explore passions and interests ❑ Make intentional choices to advance learning
Creativity **I can use my imagination to generate ideas and solutions.** ❑ Ask questions about the world around me ❑ Generate and evaluate multiple solutions and strategies ❑ Improve ideas by testing, collecting feedback ❑ See challenges and problems as opportunities to be creative	**Compassion** **I care about myself and others.** ❑ Actively listen ❑ Build relationships with peers and adults ❑ Build an extensive vocabulary of emotions ❑ Have empathy and ask questions to understand other perspectives ❑ Take action to help others	**Resourceful** **I can find the support I need to achieve my goals.** ❑ Notice and use the resources available ❑ Ask questions when I don't understand ❑ Ask for help and use resources from others ❑ Understand what environment helps me to succeed
Growth Mindset **I believe hard work will help me learn and grow.** ❑ Understand that people are not born smart and that hard work and perseverance help people achieve their goals ❑ Be willing to make mistakes and learn from them ❑ Persist when things are challenging and less enjoyable ❑ Identify emotions when faced with challenges and strategies to keep learning ❑ Seek opportunities for challenge and improvement	**Collaboration** **I can work with others to make great things happen.** ❑ Set collective goals/norms with a group ❑ Do my part to contribute to the group ❑ Respect other opinions even when different from my own ❑ Resolve conflicts in a group ❑ Seek out and work with people who are different than me	**Civic Engagement** **I can make my community a better, more inclusive, place.** ❑ Help and support others ❑ Operate with a shared responsibility to the community ❑ When I notice examples of injustice and prejudice, I take action ❑ Identify and pursue opportunities to make a positive impact in school, community, and the world

Oak Knoll School Learner Profile

As I have worked with many educators to identify the skills and strategies that support the development of the learner profile, one thing we found really powerful is curating spaces to empower both educators and students to discuss powerful examples. It is important to note that the way these noncognitive skills show up is contextual and personal. The measures of habits and skills are their best when they are informed by self-reflection, peer assessment, and educator observations over time. This shows evidence of the patterns and trends that inform ongoing student development. The goal is not to check a box, give a grade, or mark a criteria as met or not met, but instead it is to help educators, families, and most importantly, students, focus on these skills and develop them in productive ways.

If your school or district doesn't have a learner profile, talk to your community, colleagues, and students about what you value most and create your own school or classroom profile that defines the knowledge, skills, and mindset everyone should strive for. Make it visible and accessible for students.

Empower Learners to Self-Assess Connected to the Learner Profile

Once you break down the skills—or you do it together with your students—it is important for students to have opportunities to reflect on these skills and self-assess to gain a deeper understanding of their strengths and challenges aligned to the larger goals. Creating a self-assessment that is aligned to the profile can be a powerful tool to revisit across classes and grade levels by helping learners develop agency and motivation to grow these valuable skills and habits over time. Having a shared understanding of where students are in relationship to the goal can help you build relationships with them. This also allows educators and students to recognize and remove potential barriers to learning in a positive and constructive manner. When you know students' strengths, preferences, and potential challenges, you can better design learning environments and create opportunities that build on their interests and experiences to maximize engagement.

Highlight and Celebrate Actions Connected to the Learner Profile

It is fairly common for awards to focus on grades, GPAs, or attendance. It is less common but very powerful for them to focus on the skills that are critical to learners' success and growth in life, work, and citizenship. Imagine if students were celebrated each week or month for how they demonstrated characteristics of the learner profile, like being a risk-taker or inquirer or being open-minded. What you celebrate and acknowledge gets focused on, and if these skills are important, we have to show that we truly value them.

As a middle school teacher, I used to cut up paper and give the pieces to students when I noticed they completed a task or demonstrated a skill that aligned with our desired learner outcomes. Then, with those pieces of paper, they could enter in a raffle for a piece of candy or a sticker (yes, in middle school, and they loved it) at the end of the week. It was very informal but personal, and they rarely cared about winning; they just loved being recognized! Many teachers have students nominate their peers or recognize others on a shout-out wall. Consider how you might acknowledge students for demonstrating skills that align with your learner profile.

Reflect and Set Goals Connected to the Profile

Did you know we are more likely to achieve goals when they are meaningful to us and we write them down? Making time in the day for students to reflect and set goals can help them take ownership and develop agency. The beauty of a learner profile is not that everyone is the same; it is that everyone is unique and valued for who they are. When this is true, individuals are more driven to accomplish goals that matter to them personally.

Monitor Progress by Capturing Evidence of Learning and Growth

One of my favorite ways to document progress came from a kindergarten classroom where each month, students drew a picture and wrote a sentence to create a book. In August, it was a few squiggles and letters that were not fully legible. In September, you saw shape in the pictures and a few letters strung together. By January, there was more definition in the pictures and a few words. At the end of the year, there were ten snapshots of where the students were, and the progress over time was evident. Each series was as unique and special as each child. In reading, you could have students read a passage and record their growth monthly by reflecting on their progress. Older students can document their drafts, share their writing process, and grow in their ability to craft stories. I used to block out a day each quarter before I had to submit grades so students could reflect on what they had learned in relation to the key standards and their goals, identify key pieces that showed evidence of growth and mastery, and document it all in their portfolio. It was a great way for students to take ownership of a process that is too often taken on by teachers alone. Each year, students make tremendous progress in classrooms all around the world, and we often reduce this growth and their strengths and challenges to numbers or letters. Collectively gathering and using evidence to measure progress can show us what the learner can do and provide multiple means of representation.

Share Evidence of Growth in Academics and in the Skills, Habits, and Mindsets Outlined in the Learner Profile

Beyond academics, we can also help learners reflect on their skills and habits. When learners are at the center, you can focus on growth and progress over time and acknowledge the strengths and areas for improvement for each individual rather than as a class or cohort. Technology can make this easier and more visible. There are many tools that can help students document and share their learning process and their development of key knowledge, skills, and mindsets over time. These eighth-grade résumés from Vista Innovation and Design Academy (VIDA) are one of many great ways students can highlight who they are and their accomplishments and develop some great communication skills while they are at it.

Vista Innovation and Design Academy Eighth-Grade Résumés

Ignite Curiosity, Develop Passion, and Unleash Genius

The difference in Zack's experiences was not the standards, accountability systems, or resources; it was an intentional choice to focus on learners and learning first, then design their systems, policies, and learning experiences to meet them where they were and mold them into the unique and special individuals they were becoming. As a learner, he experienced a shift from a school-centered paradigm to a learner-centered paradigm, which is possible in each and every classroom. Teachers in many types of schools use these strategies and more to empower learners, and I can't wait to share them with you throughout this book.

I am incredibly grateful for the teachers who have helped both of our kids love school, feel more confident, and develop the skills and mindsets they need to thrive. The impact of a teacher who sees their students as individuals, who gets to know them and cultivates their creativity and curiosity while developing academic skills, is invaluable. When we focus on learners and connect to their interests, needs, and goals, we can create experiences that ignite curiosity, develop passion, and unleash genius.

As Zack and so many young people experience benefits from their teachers, it is clear that it's not the programs or resources that make the difference in the lives of students; it's teachers who look to learners and evolve their teaching methods in the pursuit of providing optimal learning experiences that meet their needs. This starts with the belief that all of us have genius and talents worth cultivating and the desire to create models of learning that provide opportunities to do so.

PUT IT INTO PRACTICE

Jot down your ideas and share them with your colleagues near and far. **#EvolvingEducation**

QUESTIONS FOR CONSIDERATION

How might you use an existing learner profile or design a new learner profile for your context?

YOUR PLAN:

How might you help learners understand their strengths and opportunities for growth?

YOUR PLAN:

How might you help learners set goals, track their progress, and share their growth over time?

YOUR PLAN:

CONNECT WITH LEARNERS

Relationships and SEL are secondary to learning.	→	*Relationships and SEL are the foundation of effective learning communities.*

Do you remember your first year as a teacher? Do you remember the hopes and dreams you had and also the fear? This mix of fear and exhilaration is natural, but too often, we are taught to respond to fear with control, to retain power over kids in order to keep things running smoothly. We're taught the "never smile until Christmas" rule rather than how to create a warm, inviting culture. What if we spent more time focusing on connecting with kids and creating a space where they feel safe and valued instead of demanding compliance? What if we greeted students on day one with smiles and compassion?

Sheena Carmela Juliano shared a story with me in her final year of college as she was completing her student teaching. Despite her visions of being a primary teacher, she was placed in a fifth-grade classroom and feared that the young adolescents would disrespect her, not listen, and be taller than her. One of her students, Shane, immediately made two of those fears come true (he was shorter than her, at least). She was assigned to work with Shane because he needed help with math. Shane was witty and energetic, qualities she'd been taught to see as a potential hazard for a teacher. She'd been warned that kids like Shane usually created more behavior management problems. As she tried to assert her authority from the start, his behavior turned into a mischievous and persistent noncompliance.

"Stop talking during directions."

"Get back to work."

"What are you supposed to be doing right now that you aren't doing?"

She recalled, "He'd just smirk and crack another joke." She tried to apply what she learned about behavior management from her methods courses, yet nothing seemed to work. Use proximity so he could get the hint? He didn't get it. Publicly highlight another student doing what she wanted him to do? Not quite effective. Directly give him a look? Effective, but not long lasting.

The power struggle grew each day, and as she tried all the classroom management strategies she had learned, nothing seemed to work. Then one day, things changed. While she assisted students, Shane and a couple of other students were goofing off. *Typical Shane*, she thought. While she was about to make her way over to the other side of the classroom, there was a shy nudge behind her. "Um, Miss Juliano. Can you help me make mine, please?"

Cue the record-scratching sound effect. She wondered, *Did Shane really ask me, politely, to help him?* Sheena had only seen him for his behavior and as a problem up to this point. She acknowledged, "The tired, fed-up-with-his-behavior part of me wanted to bring up how he should have been paying attention. But I just couldn't let that part win." Instead of exerting power over him and berating him for his behavior again, she opted to connect and help him and said, "Of course! Let's do it together."

That small moment fueled a deeper connection and relationship that paved the way for fewer battles and deeper learning. In the days that followed, Shane began to open up a little more. What used to be

"I don't have my math book today" started to sound like "I forgot it at Dad's house because I slept over at Mom's last night." The unsigned planners and progress reports were given exceptionally later due dates because "Mom left for a work trip, and I stayed with Grandma this weekend."

She reflected, "The more I thought about it, the more I realized that kids weren't just kids. Kids were actual people. Mini versions of people going through life the same way as everybody else, the same way that I was." From that point forward, her view of all of the students in that fifth-grade classroom changed dramatically. They weren't just kids who couldn't behave themselves or who were acting out on purpose. These were kids whose lives she knew nothing about once they walked out of the classroom door.

"I wanted to give up on Shane because I thought there was just no way for me to connect to him, but I was wrong. I let the frustration and insubordination hold me back from being empathetic and open-minded. I let the anger and high expectations restrict the warm and understanding parts of me. I let the door that I tried so desperately to shut as a form of authority in the classroom act as a barrier between me and the students."

As teachers, we have to understand that there is so much more to our students than what we see in our classrooms. What if we spent time getting to know our students and connecting to them as people instead of looking at them as the unwanted behaviors we respond to? It is crucial for all of us as we create space for students to bring their whole selves into our classrooms. Sheena's experience with Shane is a reminder of what Pam Leo says: "Either we spend time meeting children's emotional needs by filling their love cup, or we will spend time dealing with behaviors caused by their unmet needs."[1] We spend time either way, so we must decide which approach is the most beneficial to help us achieve our goals.

Connection Before Content

When I hear pushback against prioritizing relationships with students, the argument is usually that our job as an educator is not to be friends with students, it is to teach them. The focus on relationships feels fluffy, for lack of a better term. But building relationships with students and creating an inclusive community where learners feel safe socially, emotionally, and academically is central to learning. Researchers from Northwestern University looked at data, including standardized tests and climate surveys, to compare the performance of students who attended public schools in Chicago. Their main finding was that "for a range of outcomes including absenteeism, school-based arrest, high school graduation, and college enrollment, students were actually better off attending high schools that were shown to inculcate social-emotional traits rather than those that maximized test score growth."[2] If our students and their success is our main goal, we can and should focus on both relationships and learning. Like with Sheena's example, until she got to know her students and understand their experiences, there was a barrier that was impeding their learning and growth that could only be broken down by their relationship.

Most educators know in their hearts and have seen in practice that there is far more to teaching than success on a test. To ensure meaningful learning, we have to know the learners, help them understand and leverage their strengths, identify and work toward goals that matter to them, and ensure they persist through challenges and setbacks. You can't do this without building relationships first and maintaining them throughout the learning process.

Social and Emotional Learning

In *Permission to Feel*, Marc Brackett writes, "It is one of the great paradoxes of the human condition—we ask some variation of the question, 'How are you feeling?' over and over, which would lead one to assume that we attach some importance to it. And yet we never expect or desire or provide an honest answer."[3] You might want to go back and read that again and again. It's so true. How often do you respond to this question with more than "fine," "good," or "busy"? So often, it can feel as if we are on a hamster wheel: get up, get ready for work, rush off to work or get the kids to school. When we get to school, we are busy and need to get through it all so we ask but rarely make the time for honest answers. It's also hard to deal with the real answers sometimes, so we just say we are fine and stay busy to avoid how we really feel.

One thing I have realized as a mom is that if my kids are frustrated and struggling, stopping to talk about it—or as Brackett calls it, being an "emotion scientist"—in order to understand and deal with the emotions is the most important thing I can do as a parent, and it is critical in our classrooms, too. Acknowledging and making space to feel loss and sadness and moments of joy and happiness is more relevant than rushing through the lecture or more important than finishing the math worksheet. If we don't make space to feel in our classrooms and we instead expect kids to bury their emotions, then we will miss out on providing the tools and experiences to manage them, and we will fail to reach them in ways that enable us to teach them as we are called to do.

In his book, Brackett described being a C or D student despite his intelligence because he was dealing with so much trauma, including being bullied in school, abuse by family, and feeling like he didn't belong. Especially as a child, when you long to belong to your friends or family, that often supersedes the five-paragraph essay or the algebra test. You can't function, focus, or concentrate when your basic needs are not met. This doesn't mean that every time you have a bad day you should be excused from school or work, but it does mean we have to acknowledge this connection and tend to our emotions and their impact on our attention in order to learn. Attending to students' sense of belonging and ensuring they have the tools and space to discuss and regulate their emotions and challenges won't distract from our curriculum; instead, it will allow students to engage in it more productively.

Emotions Impact Our Decisions

Emotions are contagious, and as educators, our emotions impact our students and our classroom culture, so as we are teaching our students to identify and regulate their emotions, we must also practice and model this, too. In fact, our emotions impact how we show up, interact, and even how we grade. The Yale Center for Emotional Intelligence conducted a study where scientists randomly assigned teachers to two groups: good mood and bad mood.[4] One group was instructed to think about a good day, and the other group was instructed to think about a bad day. Next, they were asked to grade the exact same papers. The bad mood group scored the papers one to two full grades lower. Even worse was when the teachers were asked whether or not their mood affected their grading: 87 percent said their mood had no impact.

Although their emotions clearly shifted how they graded the same content, they were unaware or unwilling to admit it. When I suggest that grades are subjective, even with a rubric or clear criteria, this is often met with resistance, but the reality is we interpret the world differently based on our state of mind. And our emotions don't just impact how we grade; they impact how we interact with others and the decisions we make. The sooner we recognize this and the better we understand our emotions, the more conscious we can be about our emotions in our decision-making process.

Strategies to Get to Know Your Students and Create an Inclusive Learner-Centered Culture

I remember being handed a book of policies and procedures to cover each day for the first week of school. Although the expectation at the beginning of the year (or semester) was always to cover the syllabus and get to the curriculum, I have never regretted making the decision to minimize the policies and maximize the time I spent building relationships. The following ideas are foundational to developing relationships and creating a classroom culture where learners are seen and valued.

Designing Community-Oriented Spaces

The educators at Design39Campus in San Diego, California, have intentionally created open, inviting spaces where learners have the freedom to move, explore, and learn in the places that are most conducive to their needs. Walking through campus, you will see kindergartners cruising by with purpose, kids huddling in the corner of a class or at a table, and groups out in the common spaces with comfortable and flexible furniture recording projects or working on problems. In addition to the classrooms, they have also created a mindfulness center (which used to be their counseling office). They painted it a calming blue, added lights, music, comfortable seating, and tables, and created a space where you feel relaxed just from opening the doors. They open it up before and after school and during recess for students who are looking for a calm and safe space to sit, reflect, and play quiet games. They know that the environment matters and that students—especially middle schoolers—need places to take a time-out and be able to manage stress and regulate their emotions.

Ten Things I Need to Know about You

A teacher shared with me that he changed his beginning of the year survey from standard questions like "How many siblings do you have?" and "What are your favorite subjects?" to an open-ended list of the "Top Ten Things I Need to Know about You." Instead of static answers, such as "two brothers" and "art," he got responses like "It takes me an hour and a half to get to school each day," "My parents just got divorced," "It takes me longer to figure things out, so I am quiet, but I really do care about school," and "I love drawing." There are multiple ways to connect and get to know learners to better support them, and often it begins with asking the right questions and being willing to listen and connect.

Share Your Strengths

My husband, a tenth-grade teacher, told me that he decided to start the year by having students share their strengths after he read *Learner-Centered Innovation* (bonus points!). I loved this idea but was shocked when he told me that half of his students didn't feel like they had a strength to share. Just think about this for a minute. If students have made it through school and don't have an idea of what their strengths are, we have failed them!

Committed to getting to know his students and having them identify their strengths, he asked them to come back the next day ready to share something with the class. He shared how students came back the next day and juggled for the class, showed videos or demonstrated their dancing or skateboarding, spoke different languages, and much more. Although these students had a variety of talents, they hadn't thought of them as strengths or thought they made them special. He acknowledged that the relationships and community were instantly different, as each student was recognized and celebrated. People are more confident, passionate, and motivated to do better work when you focus on what's right with them instead of what's wrong with them. Creating a learning community that empowers learners to develop the skills and talents to manage themselves and build on their assets, rather than dwell on their deficits, maximizes their motivation, contribution, and impact.

Family Meetings

In the spring of 2020, a group of teachers I was working with decided to check in on students at their homes and bring them some resources. They thought they were connected to students and knew them well, but they learned more about their students and had deeper empathy for them after connecting with their families and seeing their homes. Their students appreciated the effort and felt seen and cared about. They shared that it was the best thing for building relationships and better understanding their students, and they wished they had done it sooner. Teachers who do home visits to get to know their new students each year acknowledge that it is an extra effort but also understand that it makes a huge impact. For middle or high school, this might only be reasonable for your advisory group, but it's still important. Although home visits are not always possible in many contexts, you can schedule a virtual call to check in with families or set up a space at school to meet up, connect, and provide resources and materials that students will need with a personal touch that will set you and the students up for success.

Empathy Interviews

Empathy interviews are a great way to listen and understand your students and their families. You can do this in person or virtually, but spending at least thirty minutes with your students is a powerful way to get to know them. You can use the following questions if you meet with families, too. Building empathy for your students and their families will help you develop stronger relationships with them so you can better guide and support them in their academic and social-emotional goals. Here are a few questions to ask:

- What are you interested in?
- What do you love to do?
- When do you feel the most successful?
- What comes easily to you?
- What do you want to learn more about?
- How do you like to learn and work with others?
- How can I best support you?
- What ideas do you have to improve our classroom (or school)?

One-on-One or Small Group Check-Ins

To ensure meaningful learning, we have to know our learners, help them understand and leverage their strengths, assist them in identifying and working toward goals that matter to them, and ensure they persist through challenges and setbacks. You can't do this without building relationships first and maintaining them throughout the learning process. In lieu of regularly scheduled class, could you take time to connect with each student? During virtual learning, both of my kids' teachers scheduled regular check-ins, and I did this in my graduate school course as well. These thirty-minute check-ins changed the dynamic of teacher-student relationships, and it is something I will do moving forward with every class, whether it is virtual or face-to-face. Scheduling time to connect with each student and learn more about their circumstances, goals, and ideas created a different dynamic that built empathy and allowed for more personalization and meaningful connection. Students also recommend reaching out via text, calling them, or just checking in every so often to make a personal connection. The frequency might vary based on your context. Some could do weekly check-ins with small classes or in advisory settings. In middle or high school, maybe you could schedule quarterly meetings. I encourage you to try it out and find a way to incorporate this in your schedule in a way that works best for your context.

Teach and Use Emotion Vocabulary

The Mood Meter is an evidence-based grid of emotions that helps identify the "coordinates" to your current emotional state based on pleasantness and energy. The following description represents each of the quadrants.

- **YELLOW ZONE** (high energy, high pleasantness): pleasant, happy, joyful, hopeful, focused, optimistic, proud, cheerful, lively, playful, excited, thrilled, inspired, etc. Links to heart-mind quality, alert and engaged.

- **GREEN ZONE** (low energy, high pleasantness): at ease, calm, easy-going, secure, grateful, blessed, satisfied, restful, loving, balanced, comfy, cozy, carefree, mellow, thoughtful, serene, etc. Links to heart-mind quality, secure and calm.
- **RED ZONE** (high energy, low pleasantness): peeved, annoyed, irritated, worried, frightened, jittery, tense, troubled, angry, furious, panicked, stressed, anxious, etc.
- **BLUE ZONE** (low energy, low pleasantness): apathetic, bored, sad, down, uneasy, miserable, depressed, disheartened, exhausted, hopeless, alienated, despondent, despaired, etc.[5]

Many teachers use the Mood Meter to check in with students, have them identify where they are walking in the door, or to help them self-assess their emotions. The Mood Meter is about helping people (students and adults) name and identify their emotions so they can become more aware of the impact of their feelings and choose an appropriate response. You can use this as a daily check-in, or you can use it to debrief big events. Amy Fast, author and high school principal, shared on Twitter how the Mood Meter helped their community debrief the attack on the Capitol on January 6, 2021.[6] Social studies teachers facilitated a discussion and allowed students to use the Mood Meter to reflect and share how they were feeling. They used the colors associated with the quadrants to identify and name their feelings. Having a shared language or set of images to talk about feelings can help build community, shared understanding, and support to process emotions appropriately.

Establish Classroom Jobs

As a teacher, I loved having classroom jobs. I created a list, and students applied for the ones they were interested in. I tried to match the kids and the jobs, and they typically got one of their top three choices. This created a sense of ownership for the students, and they were empowered to take on responsibilities that helped make the classroom learning community function. Students had jobs like classroom photographer, greeter (for guests), birthday celebrator, and historian. We even had a poetry reader who would kick off class, and this ended up being a saving grace. Students would stop to listen to their peers, and I never had to quiet the class, especially when coming back from lunch. In a remote or hybrid setting, there are different yet still important jobs, like having helpers get class started with a connector activity, take attendance, manage the chat, or check in on friends. There are so many ways students can help!

Learning Circles

One way I love to connect learners is through learning circles or collaborative groups. It can be a text that they read or a common challenge they are working on, but they meet regularly to check in and learn together based on your goals and objectives or theirs. This can be done virtually in small breakout groups that you manage, or kids can set up groups on their own.

The teacher plays a pivotal role in connecting with individual students and their families while also creating a community where students can develop relationships with one another. The first few weeks of school are crucial as we get to connect with students, and as a teacher, remember that as the role of the educator evolves, human connection and guidance will become increasingly more—not less—important.

Show and Tell

Show and tell doesn't have to stop after kindergarten. A high school teacher from Singapore I connected with at a conference shared how she initially built a community by having students bring something to share, and she continued to build on this practice once they felt comfortable with one another and speaking in front of the class. Next, they picked a topic they wanted to discuss from current events and practiced speaking, listening, and connecting by sharing things they cared about. When she wanted them to discuss their literary analysis, they were already connected, had built confidence, and were able to share their ideas within an inclusive learning community. Creating a place for students to chat and share what they are learning and doing in an asynchronous way can be a great way to connect kids without having a set meeting time. Creating a place for learners to share ideas, class challenges, or pictures can build a learner-centered classroom community.

In Encinitas Union School District, the sixth-grade team at Flora Vista Elementary School has created a learner-centered culture, and on one of the walls is a "Love" board where students can bring in things they love and are passionate about to share with the class. The wall is full of pictures and quotes, and it is inclusive of the identities and interests of the diverse students.

Connect Beyond the Classroom

Another terrific way to personalize each student's learning experience is to give them the opportunity to make connections beyond the classroom. Not all students have access to social capital or networks. There are many people who can serve as mentors, experts, and critical friends to bring different experiences and expertise to your students and provide invaluable access and opportunities. As Julia Freeland Fisher argues in her book *Who You Know*, "Discussions about inequality often focus on achievement gaps. But opportunity is about more than just test scores. Opportunity gaps are a function of not just what students know, but who they know. Relationships play a central role in young people's lives and all of our lives."[7] Specifically, she shares three things we can do in school to build relationships and expand networks, arguing that we can be hubs of next-generation learning and connecting.

- Integrate student support models that increase access to caring adults in students' lives

- Invest in learning models that strengthen teacher-student relationships
- Deploy emerging technologies that expand students' networks to experts and mentors from around world

A key aspect of making learning in school more personal and authentic is connecting students to other people and ideas to build and leverage their network. This means that as educators, our job goes beyond simply teaching students the content. As the world evolves, our roles are about exposing students and connecting them with experts, mentors, and others who can inspire them beyond what we know and can do.

Cajon Valley Union School District has made this a central part of their modern curriculum. Their World of Work program (#cvwow) is based on four experiences: exploration, simulation, meet a pro, and practice.[8] Starting in kindergarten, students learn about their strengths, interests, and values and connect with professionals to learn about their jobs and how they align with their own skills and interests. As Ed Hidalgo, a dear friend and educational pioneer who has spearheaded this program after spending his career counseling adults in the corporate world at Qualcomm, says, "Students can't aspire to jobs that they don't know exist." The World of Work program uses a virtual platform called Nepris that connects teachers and students to industry professionals.[9] In one instance, students at Greenfield Middle School left school for fieldwork (not a field trip) to explore a local dam. They then explored resources and completed a learning playlist at their own pace to deepen their expertise and build a 3-D model. Then they recorded a video to share the evidence. Once they had these experiences, they connected with engineers to learn more about water systems and wrote about the experience.

Another aspect of the modern curriculum in Cajon Valley is its TEDxKids@ElCajon program, where students learn how to create a powerful talk and get support and guidance to identify and share their ideas—hello reading, writing, and communication standards! Each year, students articulately share their ideas on topics including coping with grief, healthy kids, the importance of bees, and living as an only child. Through their modern curriculum, Cajon Valley Union School District is intentional about teaching students that they matter, connecting them to people and ideas, building their network to include professionals and mentors, and ensuring that other people know who they are and what they know.

Connection Is the Foundation of Learning

Connecting with students and building a learning community is not the only goal of education. We must go beyond relationships and teach students so they learn, practice, and grow. But as Sheena learned early in her career, if we don't prioritize getting to know our students, we will have a much harder time growing them. Our relationships and connections are built and sustained over time through opportunities to connect, discuss, and do things that matter. Connecting with learners is foundational to the learning and long-term impact that we as educators aspire to have. When we make the time to build relationships, we can connect students with peers, mentors, and ideas and help them thrive as learners based on who they are now and who they aspire to become.

Our relationships and connections are built and sustained over time through opportunities to connect, discuss, and do things that matter.

PUT IT INTO PRACTICE

Jot down your ideas and share them with your colleagues near and far. **#EvolvingEducation**

QUESTIONS FOR CONSIDERATION

How might you guide learners to understand their strengths, interests, challenges, and goals?

YOUR PLAN:

How might you learn where students are socially, emotionally, and academically?

YOUR PLAN:

How might you help all students feel valued and included in the classroom?

YOUR PLAN:

How might you connect students to mentors, experts, and experiences beyond the classroom?

YOUR PLAN:

BELIEVE IN LEARNERS

Learners are sorted and ranked. → *Everyone is capable of learning and contributing in meaningful ways.*

When I went to my ten-year high school reunion, I was voted "Most Changed Since High School." I was married and working as a new teacher mentor for the Hawai'i State Department of Education. I had just finished my master's in education and was on the path to complete my PhD. I was loving my job, happy in life, and by all accounts, one could say I was successful. As it turns out, no one really expected that.

Growing up, I remember we had a gifted and talented education (GATE) program like many schools do. My best friend was always in these classes and I was not, so in my elementary and middle school state of mind, it was clear to me that she was smart and I was not. I was also keenly aware of the cool projects and awesome teachers she had in these programs that I did not. There were tests that sorted and ranked us, and I let the results of those tests determine what I felt I was capable of—and so did many of the adults. As a result, I convinced myself that I was "average" and wasn't capable of anything better, so I never worked very hard to exceed the expectations placed on me. I maintained a B average because that was what was required in California to drive as a teenager and keep your car insurance reasonable, and because that was what my parents expected. I did what was required for the B and never really went above and beyond to challenge myself. Upon reflection, it is very clear to me that I had a fixed mindset about intelligence and what I was capable of.

I was recently asked about my trajectory from middle school to college, and I reflected back on my experiences in school and the impact of my low expectations for myself and those others had of me. I now realize how they influenced me tremendously. When I was in sixth grade, I tested into an advanced math class, so I left my sixth-grade class and was in a class with seventh graders and some eighth graders, but I still did not feel like I was "smart" because I didn't make it into GATE. It was hard and challenging, but I liked math and I enjoyed the class. I don't remember exactly what happened, but I moved on to the next class in seventh grade, and by the time I was in eighth grade, I had basically finished pre-algebra. When I went to register for high school, my counselor shared that the courses were going to be "very challenging" and it was also difficult to adjust from middle school to high school. Therefore, it would make sense if I took pre-algebra again instead of continuing on to the advanced classes in high school.

I trusted my counselor and enrolled in pre-algebra—again. This set me on a course to take less accelerated math throughout high school and to be on a traditional track, which I thought was fine because it confirmed where I thought I belonged. I completed the required math courses to graduate high school by the time I was a junior, and my counselor gave me the option of taking a period off or taking another math class. Like the wise seventeen-year-old I was, I obviously chose to take the period off. I was completely oblivious to the fact that there were AP classes to take, and it wasn't until halfway through my senior year, after I had enjoyed an extra lunch period with my friends, that I realized that because I didn't take an extra math class my senior year, I was not eligible to go to the colleges I had dreamed of.

Totally contrary to all of my dreams of attending a big college, I hadn't put in the work necessary and ended up going to a small college thirty minutes north of where I grew up, commuting to campus every day. Not having been in a math class for a year and a half, I was placed in remedial math and had to take extra math classes to get up to credit-bearing math my freshman year. The same pattern happened with Spanish and many of my other classes. The advice I kept getting was that the transition was going to be hard and that I should just start at the beginning again—and so I did. The content never got harder, but as many had anticipated, the transitions did. Unfortunately, instead of creating support systems, like advisory or study skills, to aid me and other students with these transitions, my advisors recommended repeating the same content. Without the challenge or support, I became more and more disengaged and stuck in my fixed mindset.

I tell you all of this because I trusted my mentors and advisors, and their expectations and beliefs in me drove the expectations and beliefs I had in myself. In a system designed for efficiency, there are many ways we sort and rank students, and the tracks we willingly or unwillingly set them on in their life come with implications that we may not always be aware of.

While my story reflects examples of lower expectations that some of my teachers, counselors, and peers may have had of me, I want to acknowledge other examples of how students are held back that include bias related to race, gender, attitudes, socioeconomic status, disabilities, peer groups, and more. For example, in a parent-teacher conference we were told that although Zack had a lot of good ideas, he was rarely the first to raise his hand or respond, and he wasn't often perceived as smart (yes, she really said this). When my mentor observed me as a young teacher, she told me that I had called on girls to answer questions twice as often as I called on boys. I was totally unaware and had to address this in my practice while also intentionally looking for other areas of bias that might be impacting my students. Additionally, a recent study in England found that in one in ten cases, a teacher's feelings about a student had a direct influence on their toughness when grading.[1] Factors that are not always related to content, such as neatness of writing and length, influence teachers' perceptions and can inflate or deflate grading.

The subtle (and not so subtle) comments, judgments, and redirection from adults has more influence than we often realize. Research shows that teachers have lower expectations of Black students and students of lower socioeconomic status, which can impact their beliefs and trajectory.[2] In Michelle Obama's memoir, *Becoming*, she recalls her counselor telling her, "I'm not sure that you're Princeton material." She continued, "Her judgment was as swift as it was dismissive, probably based on a quick-glance calculus involving my grades and test scores. It was some version, I imagine, of what this woman did all day long and with practiced efficiency, telling seniors where they did and did not belong. I'm sure she figured she was only being realistic. I doubt she gave our conversation another thought." Michelle Obama chose not to believe her counselor and worked very hard to prove that she was, indeed, Princeton material—and then some.

Strategies to Address Bias and Beliefs

If these examples are hard for you to read, I totally understand. As educators, this goes against what we are called to do in our role. And still, despite our best intentions, these examples are only a tiny window that highlights how beliefs and snap judgments impact how we see students, how we sort them, and ultimately how we influence the trajectory of their lives for better or worse. Luckily, once we are aware, we can be intentional about improving.

Check Your Assumptions

In 2016 at the San Diego County Office of Education Equity Symposium, I got to hear Liz Murray, the keynote speaker, tell her story about growing up homeless and ultimately graduating from Harvard.

Through her incredible life story, she highlighted that the experience of an individual isn't black and white. She shared many struggles of growing up with parents who were drug addicts but also the love she had for her family. It is easy to put people in a box or a special class, like "low performing," "low socioeconomic status (SES)," "gifted," "language learner," and so many other labels and categories we use in education that fail to tell the whole story of the young people in our classes. There are strengths and opportunities that exist alongside great challenges for all of us.

There are strengths and opportunities that exist alongside great challenges for all of us.

Liz shared a specific story of how a researcher tried to convince her that she had suppressed her anger because she chose not to blame her parents. After listening to him and his research, she responded, "You can read and research anything you want, but it doesn't replace my experience." Her point, which is important for all educators, was that just because the trends in research tell us that groups of people tend to act a certain way because of their experiences, or even that specific strategies are better for specific learners, doesn't mean there is a substitute for getting to really know people and all their complexities to determine the best way forward. We can learn so much by trying to see the world through our students' eyes and understanding who they are and who they can be.

We can't assume that we know individuals or understand their experiences because we have read the research or because they fit into a specific category in our minds.

Think of some these assumptions that are made often based on conscious or unconscious biases we hold:

- They aren't the first to raise their hand, so they must not get it or be that smart.

- They are always the first to answer, so they must be really smart.
- He has terrible handwriting; he must not care about putting in the effort.
- She comes from the "bad part of town"; she's going to be trouble.
- He is not capable of being in advanced placement classes.
- He doesn't have any support at home. Nobody cares about his education.
- They don't do their homework, so they must not care about succeeding in school or life.
- This is too hard for these kids; let me make it easier.
- She is a girl; she can't do advanced math.
- Those kids are smart; they need a challenge.

I was first educated about the different opportunities that exist for different students when I read *Savage Inequalities* by Jonathan Kozol, but I gained a deeper understanding when I lived it. Our education system is founded upon a system that was designed for inequitable access to opportunities, resources, and a high-quality education for each and every student.

One area of disparity I noticed early on as an educator was discipline. I grew up in a middle-class neighborhood and attended our neighborhood public schools. Students were suspended on occasion, there were fights, and I certainly had my fair share of detentions for being late. But the police were rarely, if ever, involved with students. I was very surprised to find that in the school I taught, where the population was 90 percent students of color and a high percentage of students received free and reduced lunch, police were called regularly for infractions that would have only warranted in-school detention in the schools I attended. When one of my students was arrested in middle school for fighting, I was beyond devastated. I talked to my students in seventh grade, and they were unfazed. They were used to being treated that way, and as one student, Ashley, told me, "Nobody expects anything of us."

At the core of learner-centered education is the learner, and to mitigate the challenges our most marginalized students face, we have to constantly ask questions like:

- Who gets in trouble the most? Why?
- Who is this model serving? Who is it not?
- Who is not represented in this curriculum?
- Whose values and perspectives are privileged?
- How might we open doors to more opportunities that they may not have access to?
- Is there a better way to meet this learner where they are?

Being aware of our assumptions then interrogating our practices can help us create more equitable access to opportunities for all students.

Why Believing in Students Matters

How we see kids matters more than many of us realize. Harvard professor Robert Rosenthal performed an experiment to test how teachers' expectations affect student performance. Here is how the study was conducted:

1. Researchers told elementary school teachers that they could determine which students' IQs were about to increase rapidly.
2. Students were randomly selected and labeled as "potential growth."
3. Teachers were told that these students showed potential for growth.
4. Students' real IQs were tested at the beginning of the year as well as at the end of the year.

Here is what the study concluded: "If teachers had been led to expect greater gains in IQ, then increasingly, those kids gained more IQ."[3]

This means that when students had been labeled "potential growth" and their teachers treated them as such, their scores increased. This

Our expectations—whether high or low—are likely to create results to match.

research underscores how teacher expectations (positive or negative) affect students in the classroom. Our brains make generalizations to make sense of the world. Our expectations—no matter if they are high or low—are likely to create results to match. The following diagram highlights the cycle that is put in motion by a teacher's beliefs in students.

WHY BELIEVING IN STUDENTS MATTERS

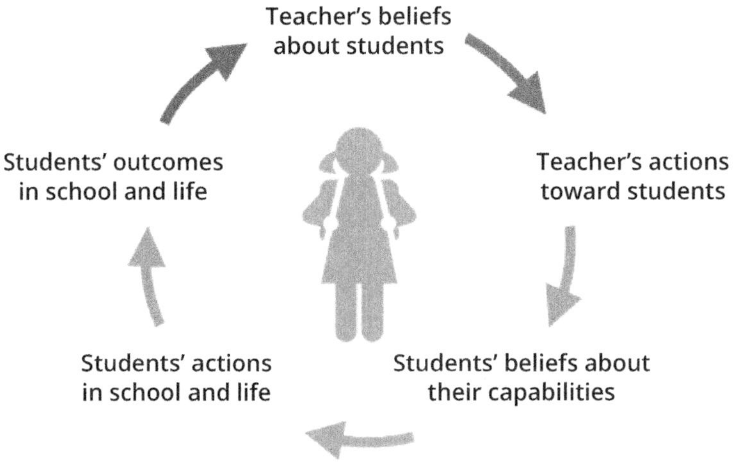

Teacher's beliefs about students

Teacher's actions toward students

Students' beliefs about their capabilities

Students' actions in school and life

Students' outcomes in school and life

It is easy to collect data and identify people by their grades, test scores, race, or gender, but we have to remember that these factors don't tell the whole story. In a 2009 TED talk called "The Danger of a Single Story," Chimamanda Ngozi Adichie articulated how "the single story creates stereotypes, and the problem with stereotypes is not that they are untrue, but that they are incomplete. They make one story become the only story." The truth is we all belong to many categories and have vast experiences and jagged profiles that make us unique. When we oversimplify identity, a culture is created where differences in the classroom are not valued and are seen as a challenge to deal with rather than welcomed assets. To go beyond labels and cultivate a sense of belonging and purpose, we must create the opportunities to get to know learners, as well as their passions, challenges, and goals, and allow them to show up as their whole selves.

Asset Framing

Narratives shape how we think and make sense of the world. Our minds also seek to confirm facts that align with the stories we subscribe to. To emphasize this point, Trabian Shorters, CEO of BMe, asked a workshop group I participated in how familiar we were with common statistics regarding Black poverty or incarceration rates. All our hands went up. He then asked how many of us knew the statistics for Black-owned businesses or military service. No hands went up. Shorters shared a different narrative, a data-driven profile of the Black community that highlighted the ways in which community members are patriotic, entrepreneurial, engaged, and generous. He gave us a data-informed alternative to the dominant story.

Think about how often we talk about students in terms of their deficits rather than their assets:

Deficit Framing	Asset Framing
Defines people by their problems	Defines people by their aspirations or contributions
Example: He is an at-risk youth who is failing two classes.	Example: He is an ambitious student who faces barriers due to endemic social and institutional issues.

When students don't do homework, when they act out, or are apathetic in class, we can assume they don't care. Even from well-intentioned educators, I still hear too often that those are the "bad kids" or "these kids don't care." Instead of assuming that students don't want to learn, could we ask, "What might be preventing students from learning in school?" All too often, as test scores, report cards, and behavior reports are gathered and analyzed, students are grouped by their deficit-based characteristics—special needs, challenging behavior, disengaged family, slow, etc.—without focusing on their strengths or their needs and goals as an individual. Take a minute to think about the categories and labels we might use in charts or conversations and consider if you would be comfortable addressing a student or their family with these labels. I certainly wouldn't.

Can you imagine a staff meeting where teachers were separated by their observation scores, social-emotional needs, or behavior? Can you imagine walking into your colleague's classroom and telling them all the things they are doing wrong? I hope not! I would also imagine you would not welcome it if your colleague did this to you, either. So, why are we OK with defining students by their challenges and grouping them accordingly? Instead, if we are learner-centered, we would start with getting to know each learner to discover what assets and strengths they bring to the table.

Set High Expectations for All Learners

When we see all learners for their strengths and use asset framing, we are more likely to set high expectations. If we really want to create environments in our schools where all learners are valued and seen as capable of achieving desired outcomes, we have to begin with the belief that they are capable. Equity occurs when every learner has access and the opportunity to engage in learning experiences that are challenging, authentic, and personal to meet their desired learning outcomes. Equity is not when each child receives exposure to the same lessons and resources.

When we believe people can do something, we act in a way that makes that outcome more likely. We need to believe in each and every one of our students and help them believe in themselves so they can see what is possible. In *The Culture Code*, Daniel Coyle wrote about a study researchers conducted on feedback in middle school classrooms. They found that there was one phrase that improved student effort and performance so much that they deemed it "magical":

> I'm giving you these comments because I have very high expectations, and I know you can reach them.[4]

When students received this feedback on a paper they wrote, they chose to complete a further revision of their work more often than students who did not. Specifically, there was a 40 percent increase among white students, and a 320 percent boost among Black students. If we want to close the achievement gap and help students achieve their full potential, we have to show them that we believe in them and give them clear feedback and support to improve.

Our beliefs about students and how we communicate them is linked to Carol Dweck's work on growth mindset. If we believe that intelligence is fixed and we don't see opportunities to grow or develop learners' skills and talents, it turns out that we probably won't. On the other hand, when we believe we can learn and improve through hard work and effort, we can create the conditions and experiences that lead to increased achievement and improved outcomes.

Having high expectations means providing the support each student needs to achieve those expectations. Instead of giving each student the same assignment to read a passage and write their response, we can provide other options so students can select what works best for them. Some might prefer reading, while others prefer a video or a podcast to learn the content. You can also provide choices for how they show what they know, whether it's in writing, video, or presentation form. If you are assigning meaningful work, meaningful feedback should not come in the form of only a grade or an evaluation. Feedback is information about where the learner is in relation to their goal or target so they can eventually get there. If we set high expectations, we must also make the time for students to go deep, get feedback, revise, and do something meaningful.

While high expectations are critical, this doesn't mean we don't allow for flexibility. Life can be challenging, and you never know what is happening in someone's world and how powerful of an impact you can make by empathizing with their situation and showing them some grace. If a student needs paper or a pencil, why not just give it to them? If they need more help, more time, or just someone to talk to, consider the impact you can make by offering those supports. Hopefully someone will do it for you when you need it, too.

It Doesn't Make Us Bad; It Makes Us Human

I want to be clear: I believe with all of my heart that my teachers and counselors wanted me to be successful, and I also believe they were unaware of the bias and lower expectations they had for me. Our brains are hardwired to stereotype, which affects our understanding, actions, and decisions in an unconscious manner. It doesn't make us bad; it makes us human. It also means if we are committed to creating an inclusive and equitable learning environment for each and every student, we have to reflect on the systems we create in the name of efficiency and tradition, inspect the beliefs we have about kids and what they are capable of, and examine the barriers that exist or that we may have created. A learner-centered paradigm requires that we, as educators, examine our beliefs and biases and disrupt systems that do not serve each and every learner so we can ensure we are seeking out opportunities to remove barriers for those who are often most marginalized in school.

PUT IT INTO PRACTICE

Jot down your ideas and share them with your colleagues near and far. **#EvolvingEducation**

QUESTIONS FOR CONSIDERATION

How might you open doors for students and expand their opportunities?

YOUR PLAN:

What assumptions might you be making about students?

YOUR PLAN:

How might you use asset framing to reframe how you talk about students (or colleagues or families)?

YOUR PLAN:

How might you set high expectations for all learners?

YOUR PLAN:

CHAPTER 4

REDEFINE SUCCESS WITH LEARNERS

Success is defined by GPAs and standardized test scores.	→	*Success is defined on an individual basis; each learner has their own unique strengths, interests, and goals.*

It seems that every conversation I have comes back to ensuring that kids are successful. I get it. As a mom and an educator, I share this desire for my kids and each and every child. My fear, however, is that as we become so obsessed with the formula of GPAs, SAT scores, the "right extracurricular activities," and the elite college in our narrow view of success, we undervalue the development and experiences in life that develop the talents and strengths that make us uniquely human and enable us to not only find the right path but navigate it and re-create it again and again.

Mandy Froehlich, an educator and author, wrote a blog post entitled "I'm Not Your Ideal Graduate" that really resonated with me and pushed my thinking. She had hopes and dreams of being a lawyer and going to Harvard and, as such, defined that as success for herself. But her path ended up taking her in a different direction, and what she found on the twists and turns of navigating her path on her own terms was actual success. Her story is important for every educator to understand. She reminds us:

> We can define the ideal graduate. It's a good idea to know what characteristics we would love our students to graduate with so we can support them in their future success the best way we know how. Resilience. Tenacity. Agency. Self-advocacy. However, we also need to realize that sometimes these characteristics don't show themselves in college graduates or how society views success. They might instead be found in the journey to get to wherever they belong, even if it's not the one we would have chosen for them.[1]

When we assume there is one path to success, we narrowly define a path that dismisses some and overcelebrates others, and we miss out on the promise of fulfillment for each and every individual based on their strengths, talents, and goals.

As I have shared, I didn't go into teaching because I loved school or because it was part of my long-term plan. In fact, I didn't get into the college I wanted and ended up going to a local school I wasn't thrilled about, California State University San Marcos (CSUSM). However, I ended up having great professors, and I fell in love with school and learning and unexpectedly found my passion for teaching. I enrolled in an amazing teacher credential program (kudos to the CSUSM middle-level program that is still going strong) that modeled for me how I could create the authentic, integrated learning experiences I had wanted as a student. When there were few jobs available in San Diego because of a budget crisis, I interviewed for a teaching job, was hired, and moved to Hawai'i to teach seventh-grade language arts. I loved that job more than I could have imagined, and my first year is still one of my favorite times in my life! Years later, I became an instructional coach and a new teacher mentor, and I loved both of those roles, too, but they were never part of the plan or the scripted path. It wasn't a plan that kept me on track; it was my willingness to navigate it when I hit obstacles and opportunities that allowed me to evolve.

What Does It Mean to Be Successful?

As a mom and an educator, I spend a lot of time talking to other parents and educators. Depending on who I talk to, I often hear assumptions about the other perspective. Teachers see that students are different and need varied support and guidance to meet their goals while they feel the pressure to assign more homework. They often share that they feel like parents only care about grades and test scores. On the other hand, I hear parents talk about their frustrations with homework or how late they stayed up doing the fourth-grade mission project with/for their kid (maybe this is just in California) or the pressure to get tutors because their child is "behind." But most of all, they worry, hope, and wonder if the kids are all right.

What I have come to understand over many conversations is that we all want our children to be successful, and we are doing the best we know how as educators and parents to make that happen. In Elmhurst Community Unit School District 205 outside of Chicago, I had the opportunity to unpack the disconnect between our hopes and dreams and our words and actions. When the families looked at what they wanted compared to what they valued, they realized that their aspirations for their children were inhibited by their own beliefs and experiences. As parents, we want our children to be able to chart their own path forward, but often, we are still living by the norms of our past. I share these concerns as a parent and often wonder, *Are they happy? Are they developing the skills they need to be successful? Do they feel like they belong and can contribute in meaningful ways?* My number one goal is that Abby and Zack are happy, self-sufficient, and good people, but if I am honest, the path there isn't always crystal clear.

In the following table, I've re-created a chart the parents made at a workshop I hosted. On the left, parents listed questions they currently ask their children to gauge their academic success and reflected on what that conveyed. On the right, they wrote questions that reflected what they actually valued. Imagine if we asked young people more questions from the right-hand column.

Current Success Indicators	Desired Success Indicators
• How did you do on your test? • What did you learn today? • How was your day? • What is your grade (on a test/project)? • Did you follow directions?	• What problems did you solve today? • Were you kind today? • Who did you help or be a friend to today? • What did you do today better than yesterday? • What are you passionate about?

Race to Nowhere, a 2009 documentary, details the all too common stories of young people who are pressured to perform rather than learn deeply or question. Students are often afraid to make mistakes and are concerned that they won't succeed if they don't get the best grades, get into the best college, and make the most money. Young people are overscheduled and overtested, and their mental health is suffering because of it. Students have become more disengaged, stressed, depressed, and burned out in pursuit of "success," yet we hear from colleges and employers that these same students are often woefully underprepared for what is needed of them to be successful. Something isn't working.

Consider a common schedule for far too many young people: They get up, get ready for school, and possibly start before-school care if the family has to work, beginning school at about 8:00 a.m. They move from subject to subject or class to class as the bells sound. Everyone moves at the same pace, with teachers covering as much as they can during class and assigning homework students must complete that night. After school, they go to tutoring or after-school clubs or sports, then they go home to have dinner, after which they'll have to catch up on homework. I often hear stories of middle and high school students spending three to four hours after school doing more work to stay caught up, and those who can't are deemed as failures, at least by their grades, or are made to feel like they aren't cut out for school. But what kind of existence is this? What exactly is this preparing students for and why?

Despite what we might consider the norm in school, we all experienced the disruption of COVID-19, and although we endured many challenges, we also learned new ways of connecting and learning and expanded our mental model of what was possible. Even beyond this, we realized we spend our time preparing kids for a future we can't predict, and as we have seen, nothing is guaranteed. Maybe instead, we should be inspiring young people to create the future. As Laura McBain and Lisa Kay Solomon, educators and designers from Stanford's d.school, advocate, students' preparedness feels insufficient:

> We have to help students understand their context and capabilities in more holistic, interdisciplinary ways than ever before. We have to teach our students to become adept time travelers—to make sense of the past in order to envision new futures; to be sense makers of disparate types of information—moving seamlessly between what's known and unknown; to flex their imagination in expansive and applied ways, and to become critical and contextual thinkers. We need them to understand the equitable and ethical considerations of policy, technology, and power dynamics of systems and structures. And, all capabilities must integrate emotional intelligence and mental well-being into our curriculum as a core investment in the future health and resilience of our students.[2]

The year 2020 was "the future" for as long as I could remember. I had seen so many "Vision 2020" documents, and I have been sharing the research from the World Economic Forum on the top ten skills needed in 2020 in the workforce since 2015. The year 2020 was the future, and now it will always be the year that disrupted how we live, work, and learn. Laura and Lisa have added their projections for the skills of the future to the World Economic Forum's original list. While the need to be adaptable and navigate change is clear, many of these critical skills are still far from being the norm of what we expect our students to learn, develop, and put into action. Consider what you would add or refine, then start designing a model that demonstrates, teaches, and grows these skills in our students.

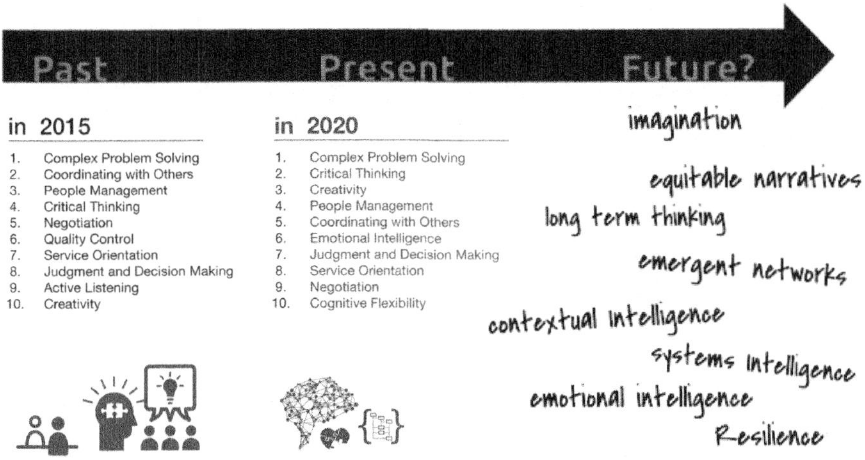

Past | Present | Future?

in 2015

1. Complex Problem Solving
2. Coordinating with Others
3. People Management
4. Critical Thinking
5. Negotiation
6. Quality Control
7. Service Orientation
8. Judgment and Decision Making
9. Active Listening
10. Creativity

in 2020

1. Complex Problem Solving
2. Critical Thinking
3. Creativity
4. People Management
5. Coordinating with Others
6. Emotional Intelligence
7. Judgment and Decision Making
8. Service Orientation
9. Negotiation
10. Cognitive Flexibility

imagination
equitable narratives
long term thinking
emergent networks
contextual intelligence
systems intelligence
emotional intelligence
Resilience

Source: Future of Jobs Report, World Economic Forum

What we have to realize as educators is these skills and lessons don't live in our textbooks, neatly packaged lessons, or worksheets; they are in our lived experiences and the world we live in. These lessons are in our communities, homes, classrooms, playgrounds, businesses, books, stories, politics, disagreements, and challenges. They are in our conversations and connections with others. What if, instead of racing through the pacing guides, we took time to explore the issues of the present, understand the complexity of our histories, and collectively shape a more just and inclusive future?

What Does Success Mean to Students?

How often do we project our own view of success on others, especially our students and even our children as parents? As I have sought perspectives about what success is for parents and educators and what it means more broadly in the education system, some of the most profound thoughts I have heard were from students on what success means to them. Student empathy interviews and surveys are a great way to learn how students think about success. At a conference I attended, educators invited a student panel to discuss a variety of issues so they could learn about the impact of their practices. The conversation quickly turned to the pressure students felt and the stress they experienced in middle and high school to keep up with their homework, sports, families, friends, and extracurricular activities. They recalled feeling overwhelmed while trying to do everything to please others. Then the question of what it meant to be successful came up.

Here are some of the things I heard from the student panel:

- Success is my parents being proud of me.
- Success is growth that I recognize and so do others.
- Success is more than test scores and grades; it's about being happy with who you are because if you don't have that, none of the rest matters.
- Success is being able to get back up when you fail.

Many teens talked about success as being able to organize their life, manage tasks, and figure out how to do it all, even in middle school. They acknowledged that they have had to learn a lot of these skills on their own and figure out how to manage the growing complexities as they moved from elementary school to middle school. Managing distractions, setting goals and priorities, tracking their progress, persevering, prioritizing time management, and practicing self-advocacy are just some of the skills students need to be successful, and they're far more important than content alone. But as the students shared, they had to learn many of these on their own. When these skills are explicitly taught, practiced, and reinforced, students are able to develop more than knowledge; they can build the skills to be contributing members of their community and lifelong learners.

Belonging versus Fitting In

How students view their success is connected to their identity and belonging. In *Daring Greatly*, Brené Brown shared what she learned about the difference between fitting in and belonging from middle school students, who might be more consumed with this than any age group on the planet, but if we are honest, a little middle schooler lives in all of us.

Here is what they said:

- Belonging is being somewhere you want to be and they want you. Fitting in is being somewhere you really want to be, but they don't care one way or the other.
- Belonging is being accepted for you. Fitting in is being accepted for being like everyone else.
- I get to be me if I belong. I have to be like you to fit in. [3]

The difference between how one behaves when they belong versus when they are trying to fit in should make us all pause and reflect. Are we creating the conditions where people feel like they belong? When young people (and adults) feel pressured to fit in in ways that are not healthy to their overall identities surrounding gender, physical appearance, race, sexuality, and other aspects of themselves, they are not at an optimal emotional state to learn, grow, and contribute meaningfully. Given what we now know about the influence of our environments on learning, it seems clear that creating an equitable and inclusive learning community shouldn't be an add-on; it is foundational to learning and living our lives to our fullest potential.

Social and Emotional Well-Being Are Central to Student Success

If we are attending to well-being, it is not sufficient to just teach the content. Instead, if we teach young people the skills to understand and navigate their emotions, manage responsibilities, and collaborate productively, they will be much better prepared to create new and better opportunities for themselves and chart their own path to success, however they define it. The Collaborative for Academic, Social, and Emotional Learning (CASEL) defines social and emotional learning (SEL) as an integral part of education and human development, and it has identified five interrelated competencies for all students:

- **SELF-AWARENESS:** The ability to accurately recognize one's emotions and thoughts and their influence on behavior. This includes accurately assessing one's strengths and limitations and possessing a well-grounded sense of confidence and optimism.
- **SELF-MANAGEMENT:** The ability to effectively regulate one's emotions, thoughts, and behaviors in different situations. This includes managing stress, controlling impulses, motivating oneself, and setting and working toward personal and academic goals.
- **SOCIAL AWARENESS:** The ability to take into account and empathize with the perspective of others from diverse backgrounds and cultures, understand social and ethical norms for behavior, and recognize family, school, and community resources and supports.
- **RELATIONSHIP SKILLS:** The ability to establish and maintain healthy and rewarding relationships with diverse individuals and groups. This includes communicating clearly, listening actively, cooperating, resisting inappropriate social pressure, negotiating conflict constructively, and seeking and offering help when needed.

- **RESPONSIBLE DECISION-MAKING:** The ability to make constructive and respectful choices about personal behavior and social interactions based on the consideration of ethical standards, safety concerns, social norms, the realistic evaluation of consequences of various actions, and the well-being of self and others.[4]

Rather than leaving the development of these critical competencies to chance, effective educators must explicitly teach these skills, help students self-assess their growth, and provide feedback and space to practice and deepen these core competencies so they can learn and show what they know and who they are. It would benefit us all to see SEL as core to success and not as an add-on. This is what high school students advocated for in a Change.org petition in which they asked the administration to broaden the path to success that's often defined by test scores and college acceptance. In this petition, the high school students pushed the adults to "start defining success as any path that leads to a happy and healthy life. Start teaching us to make our own paths and start guiding us along the way." I have seen the incredible impact that a more holistic view of learning and learners can have on the skills, confidence, and motivation of young people.

Try it out: Think about your path and the obstacles and opportunities you faced. How did this shape your journey? What did you learn from it? What might you have done differently? How might you share this with your students or children?

My hope is that students don't have to wait until college, like I did, to learn in ways that are authentic and participatory, to truly have agency and find joy in school and learning. I am grateful that my journey took me where it did and, to this day, continues to evolve into different experiences and opportunities that the seventeen-year-old me had no idea were even possible. I am extremely privileged to have had the opportunity to figure out my path and access college in ways that are not always available to learners when they don't experience success in school, when they lack the tools and support structure to navigate the complex system, and when they don't measure up based on the narrow view of success.

Success as Fulfillment

Many Americans don't believe in this narrow view of success. In fact, according to the Success Index, a landmark study by Populace and Gallup, most Americans believe in a broader view of success focused on personal fulfillment, yet they perceive others to view success as status.[5] This means the majority of people believe that success is about finding meaning, purpose, and fulfillment in life, not simply achieving high test scores and receiving access to elite institutions. However, our country's politics and policies don't often mirror this view. When louder and often more powerful people tout a narrow view of success (and create policies based on this), they drown out the silent majority.

Instead of making these aspirations of fulfillment the driver of what we do in education, the legacy of No Child Left Behind and similar policies and practices still permeate our curriculum, leadership, and view of success in many schools. In their report "Imagining September," Justin Reich and Jal Mehta describe the impact the No Child Left Behind policy had on many schools:

> Schools made dramatic cuts to the curriculum by reducing time and attention to science, social studies, civics, the arts, physical education, recess, extracurricular activities, social-emotional curriculum, and many of the things that teachers and students love about school. These cuts make room for schools to focus on test preparation for English Language Arts tests (really just reading tests) and Mathematics tests (really just computation tests). . . The costs of such an approach to teacher and student morale and to a comprehensive education are now well known to anyone who has taught during the era of standards-based school reform.[6]

In a learner-centered paradigm, how we educate young people in school can expand beyond a narrow standards-based focus—one that is optimized for developing expertise, meaning, and personal fulfillment and encourages development through authentic relationships and connections.

While you might think this sounds great in theory, you might be thinking we need to make sure individuals can get a job and be financially stable, too. Fulfillment and success don't have to be mutually exclusive, and if young people spend more time developing expertise and agency, attending to their well-being, and navigating life with a sense of identity and belonging, they will be more equipped to chart a path that can provide a productive and fulfilling life and career path.

This is in contrast to a common approach where students are exposed to a few careers and are asked what they want to be when they grow up. The answers are often influenced by early messages from adults about what is valued and what is accepted in both family and social circles. Educational psychologist Linda Gottfredson says the career aspirations of children are more heavily influenced by the perceptions of what is appropriate for one's gender and class than private aspects of their self-concept, such as their skills and interests.[7] On the other hand, when we tell kids they can be anything they want to be, we aren't necessarily helping, either. As comedian Chris Rock advises, "Tell kids the truth. You can be anything you want to be as long as they are hiring." This means young people need to understand their skills, passions, and values and how they connect with goals and career opportunities, which are also constantly evolving.

A Better Measure of Success

In pursuit of better metrics of "success" in education, I often ask educators this question: What key knowledge, skills, and dispositions are critical for learners to develop? Then I create time to discuss their answers. My goal is to make the thinking visible and align our aspirations with what really matters and with what we do each and every day in our work as educators, leaders, and citizens. You might think an answer to this question would be student GPAs, getting into the right college, or getting an A on the unit test. But no one ever says that. Instead, common responses are empathy, critical thinking, deep expertise, joy, relationships, effective communication, persistence, or some variation of these goals, as the following graphic depicts.

WHAT KEY KNOWLEDGE, SKILLS, AND DISPOSITIONS ARE CRITICAL FOR LEARNERS TO DEVELOP?

These responses align with a more holistic view of a student as a learner and a person, not a mark on an attendance record, a test score, or GPA report. Despite this infinite view of what we want and what we aspire to for our own children and students, we often are just viewing success in finite ways with short-term wins and successes that don't always add up to the actual goals that are stated in our visions and strategic plans and that live in our collective hearts.

In her book *The Rise: Creativity, the Gift of Failure, and the Search for Mastery*, Dr. Sarah Lewis writes:

> **Mastery** is also not the same as **success**—an event-based victory based on a peak point, a punctuated moment in time. **Mastery** is not merely a commitment to a goal, but to a curved line, constant pursuit.[8]

When I watch my kids in the zone and in pursuit of mastery as opposed to completion, there is a stark contrast in their efforts, energy, and motivation. When Zack is playing *Minecraft* and I hear, "I died" (which, by the way, sounds like the ultimate failure to me), he doesn't quit; he takes what he learned and rejoins his friends, and more often than not, I hear, "I died," and every so often, he will run over and say, "I won," then run back to his quest. Abby will make jewelry or some delicious treat. Some are better than others, but she keeps improving in pursuit of mastery, not a grade.

Here is an example of this in education:

- Success: GPA, college acceptance, completing assignments, A+ on the final exam
- Mastery: becoming a better writer, learning to meet the needs of each of your students, creating content that helps empower others, playing music that brings joy to the world, designing spaces where people want to gather

Mastery, according to Dr. Lewis, is more aligned with what educators and parents tell me they want for children in education, yet too often, the success metrics of test scores, GPAs, and the completion of work are what we narrowly focus on. These *are* metrics of success, but to get to mastery, we need to create the space for innovation and multiple points of failure, growth, and learning.

The problem, I think, is that when we see success as only grades or college acceptance rather than understanding these accomplishments as steps in the pursuit of a larger, more personal journey, we lose purpose. Larger aspirations of mastery will give more purpose and meaning to these short-term metrics of success that are not just a destination, but part of the greater journey that inspires learners to practice, work hard, navigate failure, and learn.

It seems a better measure of success goes well beyond knowledge and skills and includes developing deep expertise in topics and issues that matter. Success could be young people developing and using tools and practices that foster their mental, social, and physical well-being so they can thrive in their lifelong pursuits. Success occurs when individuals understand and develop pride in their identity and feel valued and that they belong for who they are. And finally, success is being able to take these skills, build on their strengths as an individual, and do something that is valuable to them and their greater community while providing a sense of purpose and fulfillment in their endeavors.

To illustrate this, I created the following diagram to illustrate this broader vision of success that includes expertise, identity and belonging, purpose, and well-being.

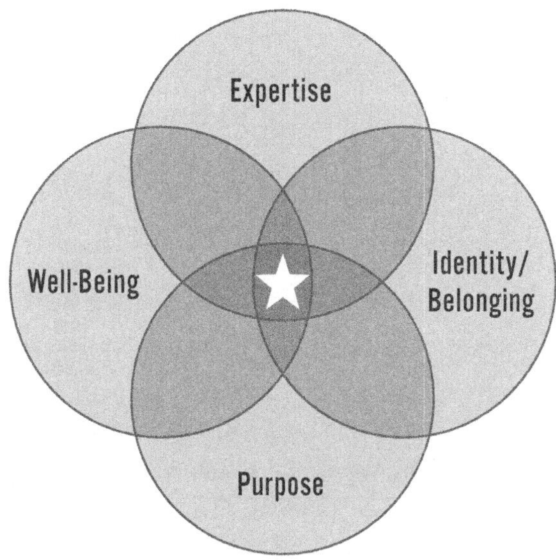

An Expanded View of Success

Connecting Our Aspirations to Practice

So how can we design a broader view of success and put it into practice? A great starting place is to create a profile of success, or, as it is sometimes called, a graduate profile, which defines what a broader view of success means to you and your community. These profiles will help identify holistic goals and guide decisions about how you design learning experiences and what resources you use. A graduate profile or profile of success helps students, families, and educators create a common vision and language to align their policies, practices, and resources. If your school or district doesn't have a profile of success, think about what you value most, talk to your students, families, and community members, and create your own classroom profile that outlines the skills you want your students to develop most.

In Logan County, Kentucky, the district worked with the community to create a common vision and created a learner-centered profile of success.

Logan County Profile of Success

Having the vision is one thing, but what is much more important is how it comes alive for learners. At Lewisburg Elementary School, one of the K–8 schools in Logan County, students strive to create experiences that help them learn and practice these learner-centered outcomes. They engage in exploratory programs to gain exposure and access to different experts and community members and do their own passion projects to explore ideas of interest and solve problems they find important. As I talked to the middle school students, many of them shared how much they loved the "Ranger Academy," which allowed all students to choose topics of interest for exploration, such as sewing, building, cooking, and community service projects. They shared with me the different student-led projects they had just completed. One group shared that they had put on a fundraiser to raise money for Ally, a student in the school who needed financial assistance for a health condition. Three girls put together a program called New Kids on the Block to ensure each new student had a person to connect and sit with at lunch, along with a welcome bag of goodies to make them feel like part of the community. Another group saw a need for their teachers' desks and workspaces to be more organized, so they worked with their teachers to build organizers.

Although they acknowledged that sometimes it was hard to collaborate with others and it could take a while to figure out how to do a project, nor do you always get it right, they learned more than just content knowledge. They loved learning about new things, working from their strengths, meeting new people, seeing different perspectives, and above all, engaging in personally meaningful work that addressed real challenges in their community. As Paul Mullins, superintendent of Logan County Schools in Kentucky, shared with me, "We aren't just creating students; we are creating better citizens." I couldn't agree more. In talking to these students, it was evident that they were already engaging in projects and learning that could help make our communities and world a better place.

Educators at Lewisburg have intentionally designed authentic learning experiences that prioritize learners and integrate the basic skills that are aligned with the standards that matter. While engaging in more authentic and personalized work, not only do students learn and improve in their numeracy, reading, speaking, writing and communicating, and critical thinking, but they are also engaging in activities that require them to use these skills in authentic and meaningful ways. This focus is on developing academic expertise, cultivating social-emotional learning, and ensuring students feel like they belong as they connect to their passions and interests. Collectively, these practices highlight the importance of teaching the whole child. The goal isn't to keep adding on and doing more; rather, it's about making intentional choices to prioritize, integrate, and do things differently based on your vision and values, with a broader vision of what success is.

Once you are clear about what a more holistic view of success looks like for learners, including developing expertise, belonging, well-being, and purpose, you can design the learning experiences to get there. We can and should teach students in ways that prepare them to be good thinkers, communicators, and critical problem finders and -solvers. With these skills, they will be more able to tackle standardized tests and other important tasks in their lives. But make no mistake: if we continue to focus on ranking students by grades, standardized curricula, and teaching to the test, valuing compliance over learning and innovation, we will continue to struggle to meet this low bar and fail to develop learners who find meaningful employment and lead productive lives.

Educators who embrace a learner-centered paradigm develop stronger, more innovative, and inspired learners. Their learning communities trust each other, and they have the resilience to thrive in an ever-changing world. Ultimately, they are the ones who will lead the rest of us into the future.

PUT IT INTO PRACTICE

Jot down your ideas and share them with your colleagues near and far. **#EvolvingEducation**

QUESTIONS FOR CONSIDERATION

What does success mean to you? What does it mean to others in your community?

YOUR PLAN:

How might you make a broader view of success more explicit?

YOUR PLAN:

What experiences might provide opportunities to put your aspirations into practice?

YOUR PLAN:

PART II

HOW MIGHT WE CREATE THE MOST IMPACTFUL LEARNING EXPERIENCES?

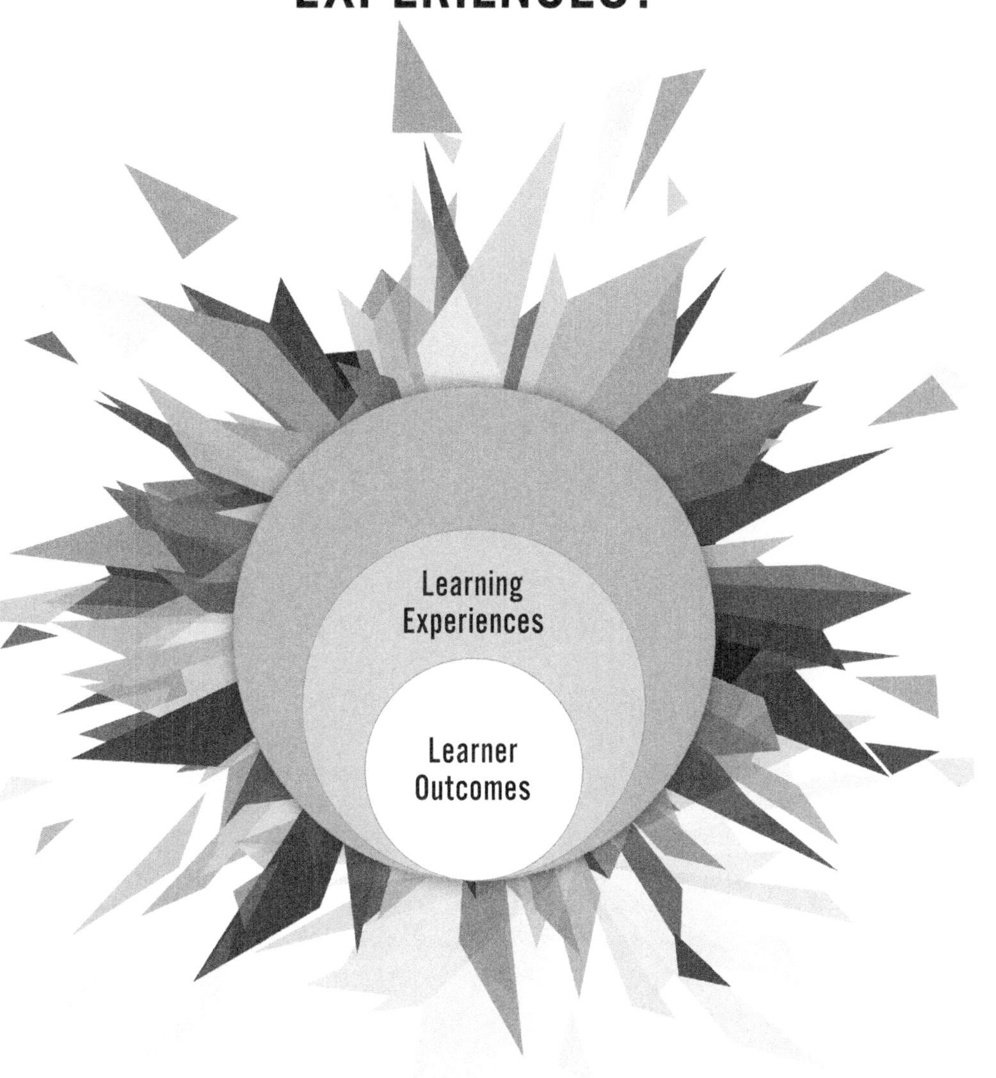

In part I, we explored who we are serving and what our aspirations are for our learners. In the chapters that follow, I have outlined four key elements of a learner-centered model and how learning sciences can inform our shift from teaching to learning. These are not meant to be prescriptive, but instead, each chapter will discuss the paradigm shifts that can help you think about new learning experiences and opportunities for your students. I will provide you with examples and strategies that I hope you will use to build upon, modify, or evolve your context to expand opportunities for all students to build their expertise, passions, and goals and learn deeply.

Chapters 5 through 9 will address the following key shifts.

From School-Centered	→	To Learner-Centered
Focus on the most effective teaching.	→	Focus on producing the most effective learning.
Learners follow a standardized path, place, and pace to assess proficiency.	→	Learners move at their pace and place and follow the path that allows them to demonstrate a mastery of knowledge, skills, and dispositions.
Learners adapt to the standardized system.	→	The system adapts to meet the needs of the learner.
Learners must be compelled to learn.	→	Learners want to learn.
Education is done to the learner.	→	Education is done by (and with) the learner.

CHAPTER 5

THE ART AND SCIENCE OF LEARNING

Focus on the most effective teaching.	→	*Focus on producing the most effective learning.*

In January of 2020, I was invited to the Encinitas Union School District Farm Lab & DREAMS (Design, Research, Engineering, Math, Science) Campus to be one of the visiting judges for the culminating event of Salad Wars, a competition in which sixth graders create, bottle, and market their own salad dressing. I got to visit the ten-acre farm (which also provides fresh produce for the district's school lunch program), and I couldn't help but smile as I watched each team's unique presentation—from Dressing Impossible whose members wore *Mission Impossible*-inspired matching uniforms, to Kaleifornia, whose brand focused on a California theme. These kids blew me away with their marketing pitches, logos, collaboration, innovation, and amazing salad dressing.

In the lead-up to Salad Wars, students spent a week at the DREAMS Campus learning about the interconnectedness of nutrition, agriculture, and ecology. Unlike my childhood experience learning about the food pyramid with a worksheet and crayons, Encinitas's sixth graders got hands-on experience learning about where foods come from and how to cultivate them. The Salad Wars curriculum offers students the opportunity to learn entrepreneurial skills as they acquire key knowledge about agriculture, health and wellness, and the environment—and have a blast doing it.

At the end of the competition, Team Saladdin was declared the official winner, but I felt like I had won. I was truly blown away by the quality of the salad dressing from each team. As a judge, I got to take home all three dressings, and my family agreed they were better than anything we had in the fridge! And best of all, this interdisciplinary, authentic project really raised the bar of what was possible in our schools and communities when we shifted our mindset from school-centered to learner-centered practices.

Salad Wars Salad Dressing

Ten Principles of Learning Sciences

Although this project sounds amazing, I can still imagine the skeptical responses: "I still have to teach students the standards!" "Learner-centered practices might be fun, but it's not *school*." Others might think such projects aren't rigorous enough, are not aligned to high-level outcomes, or are not effective for all students. However, thanks to learning sciences and brain research, we know projects like Salad Wars cater exactly to how people actually learn.

Digital Promise and the Institute for Applied Neuroscience have identified ten key insights about how people learn, along with suggestions for how to apply this information to classroom practice.[1] Throughout the rest of this chapter, I will highlight each of these principles and demonstrate how Salad Wars aligned with them.

Before we dive in, I want to acknowledge that this project, although rooted in the science of learning, is brought to life by teachers who know their students and anchored their objectives in whole-child learning outcomes, drawing on the community for resources. With these key principles in mind, let's explore how Salad Wars exemplifies a learner-centered approach.

1. *Communicating high expectations and keeping learners at the edge of their mastery helps each student reach their potential.*

Each Salad Wars team knew they would be evaluated on their pitch and would be collaborating as a team to compete against the other two teams. The expectations were definitely high and closely aligned to the math, science, engineering, and language arts standards, as well as the visual and performing arts. They pushed the level of what they were capable of through coaching and support, and they were motivated by the accountability of making a public pitch to their classmates, teachers, and invited guests. Within each group, students were able to use their strengths and interests to create their company, which not only served them well in this project but will continue to serve them well throughout their lives! I also believe that identifying exemplary work

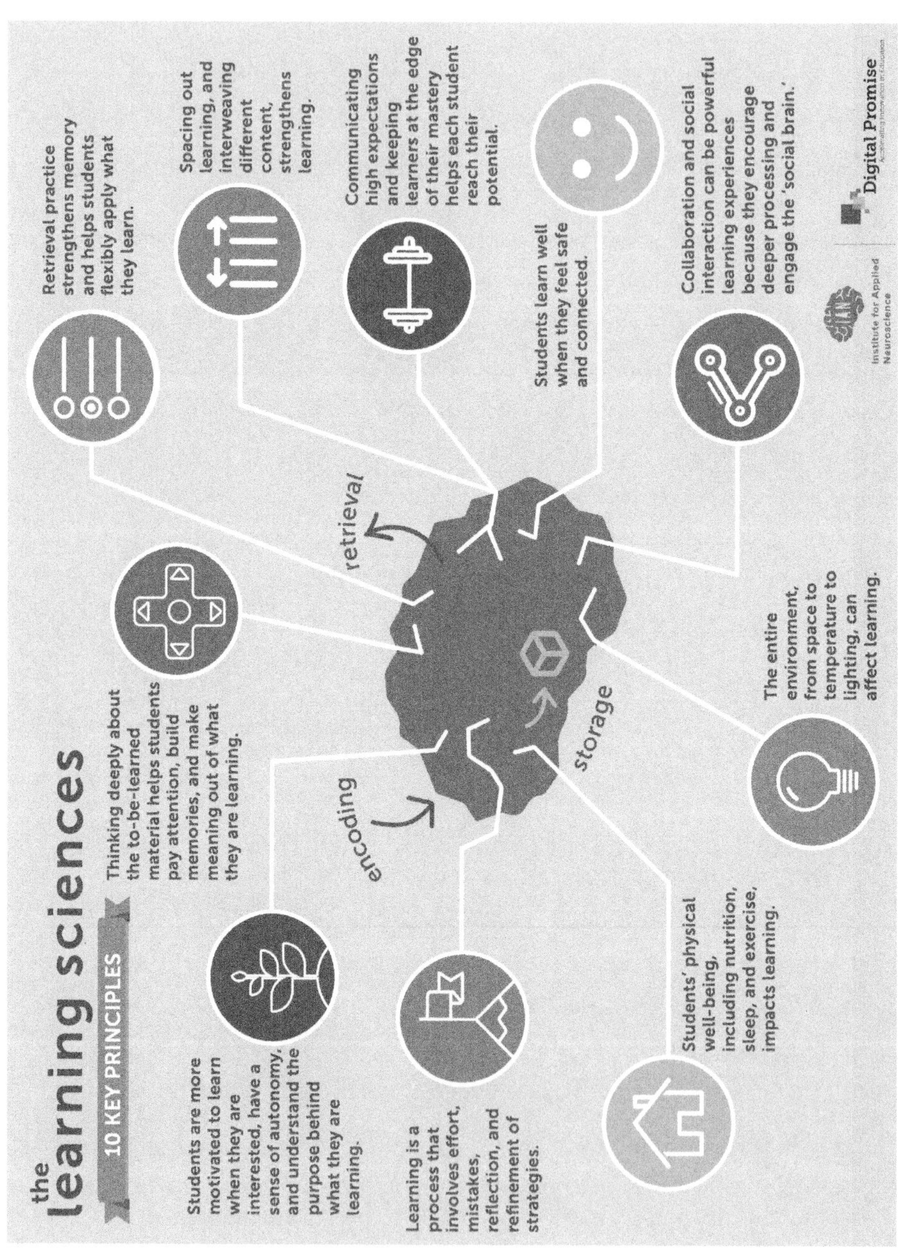

Learning Sciences Ten Key Principles

Shared with permission from researchmap.digitalpromise.org/topics/introduction-learning-sciences (e.g., models of previous students' projects) helps provide a mental model and a place to build from. Experts in their field do this all the time, and it is a useful way to clarify expectations for students in their learning journey.

In recognition of the diversity of students and their needs to reach high expectations, teachers focused on targeted, small group instruction rather than teaching to the middle (or no one). They also kept in mind the "edge of mastery" when they came up with salad dressing as a challenging and achievable product for these sixth-grade students. If they had asked them to create a line of freeze-dried products, for example, it would have likely been too difficult. High expectations and the edge of mastery is basically Vygotsky's zone of proximal development, which highlights that each learner has an optimal zone for learning that is challenging enough but within reach with effort and persistence. Finding this zone for each student takes knowing them and providing opportunities for them to take the lead and show what they are capable of. This means we, as educators, have to begin with high expectations and provide support, guidance, and opportunities to help students achieve them.

2. *Students are more motivated to learn when they are interested, have a sense of autonomy, and understand the purpose behind what they are learning.*

From the start of this project, students knew they were not just going to learn about the farm and healthy eating habits, but they were expected to create a salad dressing and design a pitch for their whole brand. They had a deadline of Friday at 11:00 a.m. to be ready to present, but they had full autonomy in deciding what kind of dressing to make, the brand identity, and the roles each student would play. The winning group, Team Saladdin, kicked off its presentation sharing, "Saladdin is a salad dressing company located in Encinitas, California, run by sixth graders at Flora Vista Elementary. We have learned to work together to ensure our dressing is one step ahead of the competition. Just one taste and you will have a whole new world of flavor." The students expressed their unique perspective with references to *Aladdin* (one of my favorite childhood movies).

We know from decades of research on motivation that autonomy and purpose are critical in learning. If we want a learner to be motivated, we need to provide opportunities that allow students to engage in authentic tasks, foster autonomy, invite the pursuit of mastery, and intrigue them with a sense of purpose. Students are more invested when they are setting goals in collaboration with teachers and peers, charting their course of action, and working along the path to mastery.

3. Students learn when they feel safe and connected.

The Farm Lab is not only a beautiful space; it is a place where students are cared about and their curiosity is nurtured. As a student shared in their reflection at the Farm Lab, "Your ideas will be respected, and you will feel connected." The teachers and administrators come to learn alongside their students, and the experts at the Farm Lab model, guide, facilitate, and mentor students as they learn about the farm and work through the design process all the way to the day of the presentations, where the adults celebrate the amazing work of the students!

The learning communities that value each learner are the ones I have seen make a huge impact on students. They create spaces for their voices to be heard, and they value and cultivate skills that help individuals and communities learn and work together.

This is a poem written by students on the Farm Lab's Facebook page, reflecting on the experience:

> Farm Lab is a great place to be.
> It's truly a sight to see.
> With haystacked surroundings,
> It's very astounding.
> We've learned many things
> And felt like kings.
> But nothing can compare to how it feels to share.

Your ideas are respected,
And you feel connected.
Farm Lab is a lovely place.
Together, we can help save the human race.
We learned a lot and can't wait to help the environment.[2]

4. *Collaboration and social interaction can be powerful learning experiences because they encourage deeper processing and engage the "social brain."*

Each student had a role in the presentation as well as the development of the company, the brand, and the salad dressing, which all involved learning key content and developing expertise. The individual accountability was central, but the joy and learning were deepened through collaboration and working together on the project. You could see how much fun the students had working together to create something more powerful than they could have possibly done alone.

Teachers can also inspire students by modeling collaboration themselves. For example, I had the opportunity to observe a lesson where two teachers collaborated to design a lesson on hydroponics. They also were able to observe the other teach. In doing so, they modeled effective collaboration and took their learning to the next level. Collaboration for adults often leads to more collaboration for students.

5. *Learning is a process that involves effort, mistakes, reflection, and refinement of strategies.*

Each team made multiple variations of their salad dressing as they experimented with various ingredients and the chemistry of the blend. Their logos, speeches, dances, and signs were evidence of the process they had gone through to design, test, get feedback, edit, and finally produce. When we only focus on the end result, we fail to communicate to learners the importance of sharing ideas early, getting feedback, and revising things to improve. If we don't honor the learning process, we communicate that we either get it or we don't. As a result, we are negatively impacting learners' confidence, creativity, and investment in their own learning and growth. Increasingly, there is a focus on failure in the learning process, and it is certainly part of it, but the bigger picture to me is acknowledging that success isn't black and white. Learning is a process, and it takes time, effort, and growth. Think of a time when you had a meaningful learning experience. Did you get it right the first time? What helped you learn and improve?

6. Retrieval practice strengthens memory and helps students flexibly apply what they know.

In spite of this research, I hear of policies where students get one chance to pass a test, with no retakes or revisions to ensure the testing environment is "fair and equal." If we look at the research on how we learn, we might want to consider other alternatives to this approach. Instead of exposing students to the same content and instructing them to submit the same assignment and take the same unit test, we could create the structures for students to understand the goals then allow them to try, learn, practice, reflect, and refine their skills to show mastery.

At the Farm Lab, students spent time writing, revising, and practicing their pitches so they could retrieve them when they were presenting their ideas. They put on a show and had choreographed parts that demonstrated what they learned in real time for an authentic audience.

7. Spacing out learning, and interweaving different content, strengthens learning.

This project brought together many different disciplines to help students create a product, and the application of these disciplines increased the connections of these concepts, as students had to switch between concepts and strategies to complete the task. I couldn't help but smile as I watched each team's unique presentation, which was the result of their hard work.

Leading up to their pitch, they learned about food production and the importance of water sources, and they studied the drought patterns in California. They then designed and built a desalination model after reviewing the drought patterns. They calculated their collected freshwater totals and reviewed their design to see what improvements could be made. Using the engineering design process, they iterated the design to improve it.

Switching between different content requires learning, using multiple strategies, and giving students time to practice. This is especially critical as students learn to use content knowledge and strategies more flexibly to transfer learning into action.

8. Thinking deeply about the to-be-learned material helps students pay attention, build memories, and make meaning of what they are learning.

When students have an authentic purpose and audience beyond their teacher to share what they are learning, they are more motivated to learn and often go above and beyond. Throughout this one-week project, students thought deeply about the ingredients of their dressing, the desalination process, and the creation of their products and ideas as part of this interdisciplinary unit, which also aligned with multiple standards, like Next Generation Science Standards (NGSS), mathematics, listening and speaking, California geography, and peer collaboration. The coordinator of this program, Julie Burton, beamed with pride as she walked through classrooms and observed the week's events, sharing, "This is not about testing kids on their knowledge of organic salad dressing, desalination engineering, or marketing; it's about providing an opportunity to gain, apply, and share new knowledge that students can carry far beyond the classroom."

I am excited to see more schools moving toward structures that empower learners to share their knowledge with projects like portfolios and student-led conferences (more on this in chapter 6). When students have to share their learning process and defend it to adults and their peers, it makes learning real and empowers them to take ownership of the process and their next steps.

9. Students' physical well-being, including nutrition, sleep, and exercise, impacts learning.

I will let you in on a little secret: I do not always react the best when I haven't eaten (or when I don't get enough sleep). My family refers to it as "hangry"—hungry and angry. Students are human, too—even the middle school ones—and they need structure, sleep, food, and movement . . . lots of movement. When students (and adults) don't get these things, they act out, fail to react appropriately, and get into trouble or disengage. At the Farm Lab, students learned about healthy eating choices so they could make informed decisions. They were also able to move, explore, and be in a healthy learning environment. This undoubtedly affected their mood, attention, and retention of information.

10. The entire environment, from space to temperature to lighting, can affect learning.

The Farm Lab was designed to foster curiosity and teach and reinforce the new lessons learned. This eco-friendly farm was designed with flexible classrooms, workspaces inside and outside, and maker labs with all the rooms named after fruits and vegetables. It was open, lacked clutter, and all the spaces were intentionally designed to use the walls, tables, and outdoor spaces for collaboration and learning. The spaces were designed to ensure that learners (educators and students) had options and choices in a variety of paths to get what they needed.

Sunlight, as well as views of nature from the classroom, can increase student achievement, well-being, and behavior. You might not be able to provide all of these things depending on your classroom, but understanding their impact can help you make decisions about opening windows or creating flexible outdoor spaces if possible. I also know that not all classrooms were designed with this research in mind. My first classroom was on the leeward side of O'ahu, which was known to get up to one hundred degrees, with no AC, so we would open all the windows to let in the trade winds, which is why every paper was weighed down with rocks. It was especially fun when birds flew in the class (#TeacherLife). We used the outdoor halls and my office to create reading and collaboration nooks for effective learning spaces and make do with what we had.

Try It Out

Think back to a time when you were learning something new that really stuck with you and made a lasting impact. How did you learn that new skill? What were the conditions? What resources did you use? Why? What practices were aligned with the research findings? What was missing? What would you add?

Addressing "Learning Loss"

Coming out of a disrupted school year due to COVID-19, I understand that there will be gaps in content knowledge, skills that have been out of practice (including social skills), trauma that will have impacted student (and adult) well-being, and more. When we put the pressure on educators and students to recoup a year of "learning loss," it is problematic for a few reasons: 1) the mindset is deficit-based and fails to help us focus on each child and what they need. 2) It puts unrealistic pressure on educators to catch everyone up since they were never at the same place to begin with. 3) It's not likely to really improve outcomes unless we do something different.

What we know about school compels us to work through the curriculum with more worksheets and tests and group kids by "ability" according to the aforementioned tests in order to catch them up. Yet, if we really want to improve outcomes for students, we have to use principles that we know actually impact learning.

Two research studies of thousands of students in diverse school systems across the US showed that project-based learning significantly outperformed traditional curricula, raising academic performance across grade levels, socioeconomic subgroups, and reading abilities.[3] Engaging in well-designed projects, like Salad Wars, can teach students how to apply what they've learned while also showing they are able to demonstrate it on a test as well.

Creating Alignment between Research and Practice

Most of us know the basics about how to stay healthy: get eight hours of sleep, ensure proper nutrition, and get regular exercise. There is plenty of research and evidence that supports these practices. Of course, how we put these basic principles of health into practice varies for each individual. Some people prefer to run for exercise, and others like going to the gym or hiking.

Similarly, the ten principles of learning science discussed in this chapter are not meant to be prescriptive. They are ideas and provocations to ground your practice in both research and the context in which you teach. Not everyone has access to the Farm Lab, but consider the opportunities that exist in your context and how you might be able to look to community partners. This was a space that was brought to life by teachers with a passion who collaborated to design this experience for their students and community.

Regardless of your particular teaching context, we know that when learners are held to high expectations and are guided to the edge of their comfort zone, they grow. We know we all learn best when we are motivated and have an authentic purpose. Factors such as the environment and our own physical and emotional well-being influence how and what we are capable of learning. The next four chapters will highlight strategies and examples of how you can design learning experiences that are aligned with these principles to improve engagement and retention and impact students far beyond the classroom.

PUT IT INTO PRACTICE

Jot down your ideas and share them with your colleagues near and far. **#EvolvingEducation**

QUESTIONS FOR CONSIDERATION

Which of the learning science principles are your greatest strengths as an educator?

YOUR PLAN:

Which of these principles highlight opportunities for growth?

YOUR PLAN:

How might you create more alignment between research and practice?

YOUR PLAN:

How might you create a learning experience like Salad Wars that aligns with your context?

YOUR PLAN:

COMPETENCY-BASED LEARNING

Learners follow a standardized path, place, and pace to assess proficiency.	→	*Learners move at their pace and follow the path that allows them to demonstrate mastery of knowledge, skills, and dispositions.*

I once joined a professional learning community (PLC) for their bimonthly afternoon meeting. The team walked into one of the teacher's classrooms, where they chatted about the day until everyone had arrived. Once the meeting started, one of the teachers pulled up a document with four questions on it to record the minutes.

The four questions were:

- What do we expect our students to learn?
- How will we know they are learning?
- How will we respond when they don't learn?
- How will we respond if they already know it?

The teachers collectively began to look at their benchmark data, fill in the answers, and search through the pacing guide to indicate which standards they were supposed to be teaching that week, which assessments they were giving, and how they were going to reteach those who "didn't get it."

At the end of the meeting, the team of teachers had completed the task, but not one teacher kept the information for themselves; it wasn't seen as useful in their daily classroom practice. Their goal was clearly to complete the minutes to turn in and move on. This PLC was driven to complete a task, and although they wanted students to succeed and do well on the desired learning objectives, the meeting and conversations were focused solely on answering questions and submitting the required minutes.

Many administrators have leveraged resources to ensure students take regular benchmark assessments and teachers come together to analyze the data. In fact, recent insights suggest that analyzing student-assessment data is a widely practiced activity (and, often, a mandate) for teachers in the US yet shows almost no evidence in raising test scores.

Yes, you read that correctly: there is almost no evidence that analyzing student data, understanding weaknesses, and reteaching raises test scores. The report highlights research from UPenn Professor Margaret Goertz and colleagues, who observed that "the teachers mostly didn't seem to use student test-score data to deepen their understanding of how students learn, to think about what drives student misconceptions, or to modify instructional techniques."[1] How much more useful could that PLC I observed have been had the focus been on raising questions about the students and understanding their needs so they could delve into ways to improve their practice? The four questions they asked would have been great if they were used to guide and investigate practices and collaboratively explore new and better ways to meet the needs of learners. But simply answering these questions and filling in worksheets won't change how students learn or how teachers teach.

The authors articulate it this way: "Understanding students' weaknesses is only useful if it changes practice. And, to date, evidence suggests that it does not change practice—or student outcomes." Data-driven processes are intended to help identify areas of need and "fix" the weakness, but as the researchers point out, "with all the attention turned on students' weakness, no effort is made to proactively remove barriers to learning, nor are their strengths nurtured." When our data-driven practices lead us to overemphasize weakness, we miss out on everything learners bring to the table and opportunities to see them, know them, and grow them.

To be clear, I am not arguing that looking at data is not important. However, the power in using collaborative time to analyze student outcomes is not in the data analysis alone; it is in the opportunity to use various data points and engage in meaningful conversations to question, learn, and generate new ideas to impact student learning. It is important to know where a learner is in relationship to where they are trying to go, and the process works best when we can bring the learners into it. Students and teachers alike are motivated when they have ownership over the work they are doing, when the data is meaningful and they have the means and resources to solve important problems. Assessment for and as learning can be very powerful!

Do Your Assessments Impact Learning?

In their book, *Classroom Assessment for Student Learning*, assessment gurus Rick Stiggins, Judith Arter, Jan Chappuis, and Steve Chappuis remind us, "Although we haven't traditionally seen it in this light, assessment plays an indispensable role in fulfilling our calling. Used with skill, assessment can motivate the unmotivated, restore the desire to learn and encourage students to keep learning, and it can actually create—not simply measure—increased achievement."[2]

Based on this notion, I have been working with educators on assessment for and as learning to unpack some common assessment practices in school. Some assessment practices positively impact learning, and others, despite our best intentions, end up hindering the learning process.

The following chart aims to identify the general assessment practices that improve the learning process versus those that can hinder it.

Assessment Practices That Impact Learning

Hinders the Learning Process	Improves the Learning Process
• Timed tests • Lack of high-quality resources • Red marks • Communicating in grades or percentages • Isolated feedback (e.g., "great job") • Bias (implicit and explicit) • Narrow view of "smartness" • Past experiences/beliefs • No clear focus/structure • Fixed pacing guides • Tracking • Overwhelming rubrics • Deficit-focused • Conflating behavior and skills • Grading homework and practice • Averaging grades	• Transparent learning targets • Co-constructing success criteria • Relationships • Examples (strong and weak) • Self-reflection • Goal setting • Multiple attempts • Progress tracking over time • Peer assessment • Collaboration • Clear structure • Mentoring/conferring • Multiple attempts • Authenticity • Multiple ways of representing knowledge

A standardized education system is designed to move kids along a certain path in a certain period of time, and it often ignores the variability in learners and their circumstances. Data-focused assessments, such as averaging grades and tracking students based on test scores, fail to allow learners a flexible path or pace toward mastery. When students don't perform on pace, they are seen as "behind" or even failing.

Exacerbating this, grading practices often fail to communicate what a learner knows and can do. In *Grading for Equity*, Joe Feldman highlighted a principal's (Mallory) reflections as she investigated grades across the campus. Here is what he shared:

> If you were a student in two of three teachers' math classes, you had about a 20 percent chance of getting a D or F, but if

> you were in the third teacher's math class, you had a 0 percent chance of getting a D or F. In the English classes, taught by three different teachers including Ms. Richardson and Ms. Thompson, the range of D and F rates—4 percent, 22 percent, and 35 percent—was even more dramatic. Mallory double-checked the grade data, then double-checked that students in the classes weren't significantly different—in other words, one teacher's students as a group didn't have lower standardized test scores or higher rates of absences. No, the groups of students were similar; the only difference among the classes seemed to be the chances of receiving a particular grade.[3]

Students' grades varied depending on the grading philosophy of the teacher. In some classes, homework wasn't counted if it was late. In other classes, points were deducted, and in others still, it was taken late. In some classes, revisions were accepted, and in others they were not. In addition, the "weight" of homework, classwork, and tests was counted differently in each class. In schools across the world, we have educators who believe in giving no zeros, while others believe in granting no retakes. These beliefs impact the grades students get. As much as we want grades to reflect what students know and do, they often communicate what teachers value and how well students can comply with those rules.

As much as we want grades to reflect what students know and do, they often communicate what teachers value and how well students can comply with those rules.

Strategies for Competency-Based Learning

As education continues to evolve to address the knowledge, skills, and habits the world demands, assessment practices are a key lever for meaningful shifts. Seat time, grade point averages, and standardized testing have historically served as the foundations of a school-based system, but as we broaden our view of success, we must also shift how we measure it. Averaging performance on assignments, quizzes, and tests does not accurately reflect growth or what a student actually knows at a given point.

In a mastery or competency-based system, the learning goals are clear and transparent to the students, and instruction, resources, learning experiences, and assessments are leveraged to meet the learner where they are and help them navigate their unique path to mastery. The Aurora Institute, a leading organization in the field, defines competency-based education as "tailoring learning for each student's strengths, needs, and interests—including enabling student voice and choice in what, how, when, and where they learn—to provide flexibility and supports to ensure mastery of the highest standards possible."[4] Shifting the expectation from completing tasks to showing evidence of what students know can create more equitable access and opportunities for learners to demonstrate mastery in a variety of ways. Although competency-based learning requires multiple shifts in the system from policy to practice, these seeming difficulties don't have to prevent an individual teacher from making these shifts in their classroom. Like many of these shifts, it's not necessarily about doing more, just doing different. Let me show you how.

Prioritize Whole-Learner Outcomes

Lindsay Unified School District was a pioneer in competency-based learning, and it continues to evolve and provide models of what is possible. In the district's book *Beyond Reform*, its leadership team explained that assessment is tightly integrated with learning. "In the cycle of instruction, assessment is used to show evidence of learning and to shape future instruction."[5] The learner outcomes are clear, which helps learners self-evaluate, plan for advancement, and identify areas where greater support is needed. One effective strategy for communicating and prioritizing a vision that focuses on the whole child is to define the skills, knowledge, and mindsets you want learners to develop. The following table from Education Reimagined's "Transformational Vison for Education" in the US articulates some more holistic outcomes that move beyond knowledge to include knowledge, skills, and dispositions.[6]

KNOWLEDGE	
The theoretical or practical understanding of someone of something.	
• World-class standards • Career and technical education • Global competence	• Other content areas and essential literacies • Applies knowledge
SKILLS	
The capacities and strategies that enable learners to apply knowledge to novel situations, engage in higher-order thinking, problem solve, collaborate, communicate effectively, and plan for the future.	
• Learning how to learn • Time/goal management • Critical thinking • Problem solving • Working collaboratively	• Communicating effectively • Metacognition • Self/social awareness and empathy • Creativity and innovation
DISPOSITIONS	
The behaviors and ways of being that contribute to learners fulfilling their full potential.	
• Agency (self-efficacy) • Curiosity • Initiative • Resilience • Adaptability	• Persistence • Leadership • Ethical behavior and civic responsibility • Self-control

Knowledge, Skills, and Dispositions by Education Reimagined

Aligning on desired outcomes is a critical step to designing learning experiences to develop these outcomes. We can't cover it all and go deep at the same time. It is necessary to move from overwhelming lists of standards and surface-level curricula to prioritize the standards and competencies that matter most. Here are some other ways to further identify and prioritize what matters most:

- Ask your community what matters most to them, then listen.
- Prioritize desired whole-child outcomes.
- Define proficiency and clear learning targets (knowledge, skills, and habits).
- Align your resources and support with your vision.

Competency and Evidence-Based Grading

So how can we provide grades and make assessments that are more reflective of the learning that is happening and where the learner is in their journey? In his book *Get Set, Go!*, Dr. Tom Guskey identifies three types of grading criteria that he says must be distinguished in reporting student performance—product, process, and progress criteria—which all relate to academic achievement, cognitive outcomes, and process criteria.[7]

1. Mastery of Core Content + Knowledge (Product)

What have I learned?

Based on desired competencies or standards, this grade reflects the level of achievement of the desired learning goal or what students are able to demonstrate they know and can do. It's not an average of multiple scores or conflated with homework, participation, or behavior; it should simply reflect their ability to demonstrate a mastery of desired skills. For example, on a report card or progress report, you would see the competency or standard and simply "met" or "not met." Can you multiply fractions, balance equations, or analyze a text?

2. Growth (Progress)

How have I grown?

One of the things I lamented as a teacher was that my students who showed so much growth but had not yet met the standard didn't have a way to highlight their progress and be celebrated for the growth in their grades. This is often the reason behavior and effort get mixed in with mastery or performance grades, but they are actually separate areas of assessment. I can try really hard to train and run five miles and show incredible growth in my endurance and speed, but if I can't actually run five miles without stopping, I don't actually meet the standard. Similarly, my students who started seventh grade at a second-grade reading level showed incredible growth to get to fourth-grade levels in a year, but they were still not at grade level. My students who were reading at grade level but didn't put in much effort were at standard, but their growth was minimal. Both are important to track, measure, and reflect upon in the pursuit of ongoing learning and growth.

3. Habits (Process)

How do I use my skills to learn and improve?

In our lives and work, many of us seek to develop mindsets and habits, such as a growth mindset, initiative, self-direction, perseverance, planning and organization, goal setting, responsibility, citizenship, empathy, and flexibility—yet these skills are rarely taught explicitly in school. Still, Guskey found that even though these noncognitive skills are generally absent from the school curriculum and are rarely measured reliably, they often influence the grades teachers give. It's essential to separate them from the assessment of mastery because these habits can be contextual and are rarely mastered; we constantly need to practice, reflect, and evaluate the impact of these skills on our performance. Consider a scale of frequency, such as "rarely," "sometimes," and "often," rather than a mastery scale to assess these habits for progress-reporting measures.

The following table outlines how we can broaden our assessments to align with what we value and, more importantly, how we can make students an integral part of the process.

WHAT	Mastery (Product)	Growth (Progress)	Habits (Process)
WHY	What can I do related to grade-level expectations?	How have I grown based on my personal journey?	What habits and skills are helpful to learn and grow?
HOW	Performance assessments Presentation of learning Standardized assessments Rubric	Goal setting Self-assessment Standardized assessments Portfolio Progress monitoring	Rubric Self-assessment Teacher observation Portfolio Presentation of learning

Assessment can, and should, be about growing and learning instead of being punitive or used as a "gotcha" moment (I am looking at you, pop quiz). Instead, a competency-based model is about identifying the specific knowledge, skills, and habits that are valued, explicitly teaching them, and providing guidance to develop them. We can bring students into the process to reflect on these skills, get peer feedback, and provide evidence of strengths and areas of growth. With clear learning goals, we can bring students into the process to create their own portfolio, self-assess, and capture evidence of their growth with things like pictures, pieces of work, anecdotes from the playground, or group collaborations that better capture their learning journey and growth over time.

When students know the learning targets and have multiple opportunities to learn, experiment, and refine, they are much more invested. Students should be central to the assessment process, setting goals based on the course or their current performance, and should be taught to document and share evidence of their personal goals related to academic mastery, growth, and habits.

The Role of Feedback

Of course, conversation about student progress shouldn't only happen at culminating events. Feedback is critical along the way. However, many teachers are reluctant to commit to a practice that takes so much time. I love this provocation from @rlawsum, a teacher I found on Twitter: "WHAT IF I only asked students to do as much work as I could give thoughtful feedback on each week?"[8] It sounds so simple and effective, and we know this would not only save time but improve the quality of learning. Evolving in education is not just about adding; it is also about subtracting. This means being thoughtful about what you assign and why. And instead of teachers taking on the assessment and the giant workload of providing feedback after the school day, carving out time during the day and building in structures for feedback builds a sense of connection, purpose, and ownership. Here are three ways students can get and give meaningful and timely feedback without putting an undue burden on teachers.

Self-Assessment

Self-assessment allows students to take ownership of the learning process. To help students complete effective self-assessments, models of success and expectations about specific learning goals must be crystal clear. Checklists and rubrics can be really helpful, especially if they are cocreated and the students have a clear grasp of what is expected of them. Creating time to build a routine for this practice is critical for students to understand where they are and determine their next steps.

Peer Feedback

Although self-assessment is important, we may not always see the big picture, so we can benefit from approaching things from a different perspective. Peer feedback provides students an opportunity to get new ideas and illuminate blind spots. Some simple structures, such as Wows and Wonders, can help students (and adults) provide kind, specific, and helpful feedback. Structures such as critical friend protocols allow students to identify a question for feedback and have their peers ask clarifying questions to provide it. This process is helpful for the students both getting and giving feedback. As everyone becomes more familiar with learning targets and discussing work in relation to them, everyone will improve in this area.

Teacher Feedback

This is usually the most common type of feedback, but it takes a lot of time to give meaningful feedback to all of your students, and it is not always useful if all the work falls on the teachers. Five-minute conferences can be a really powerful way to check in with students and provide timely meaningful feedback based on their needs. Teachers can meet with a few different students or small groups each day to check in.

Meaningful feedback is not the same as a grade or an evaluation. Feedback is information for the learner about where they are in relation to certain goals or targets to help them get there. If we can prioritize learning goals and only assign meaningful work, we can make the time for students to go deep, get valuable feedback, revise, and produce great work.

STUDENT EXHIBITIONS: The Power of Sharing the Product and the Process

Like a musical production or a game, an exhibition is a day my son's school designated for all classes to put their learning on display, invite families in, and share how and what they have been learning throughout the semester. Exhibitions are a critical part of a project, as the Share Your Learning website highlights: "When students know they will share their work with an audience beyond the classroom, they are motivated to make it high quality. The best exhibitions showcase work that has required students to think critically, problem solve, and revise through multiple drafts."[9]

This is backed by research on motivation and has been evident in my own experience as an educator, but nothing beats the opportunity to experience this as a parent! Leading up to the school-wide exhibition, Zack constantly talked about the fantasy story he had been working on. He had memorized the first couple sentences of it and was really proud of his work. It had been through many revising and editing phases with peers and his teacher, but he hadn't finished typing it, and he wanted to work on it at home because the exhibition was on a Wednesday. Zack had always struggled with and been unexcited about the technical aspects of writing, but he was so excited about sharing his story with an audience that he put in the extra work to focus on structure, grammar, and punctuation. The public deadline allowed him to feel ownership over the writing process. Seeing how motivated he was, I couldn't have been more thrilled to work with him to finish his nine-page story. I sat and listened as he narrated the story aloud to Google's dictation tool. He then went back and revised the "red squiggles" and added punctuation where it was needed. Zack kept going because he was inspired, and technology has made it so much easier to capture his ideas. As he was working on his story, I couldn't help but think of how much he had grown in his writing and confidence in the last year. He also recognized his growth and effort as he shared, "This is my best work yet!" #ProudMomMoment

On the evening of the exhibition, the school was packed with families and students buzzing around to make learning visible and celebrate everything the kids had accomplished. Our family bounced back and forth between the kids' rooms to celebrate their work and see what other classes were working on. Abby's fifth-grade class project was "mind control," where they learned all about the brain and how it influences our actions and reactions. They made calm kits for the younger classes, discussed growth mindset, created their own learner profile, and wrote narratives about overcoming obstacles. During the exhibition, Abby taught us about a growth versus fixed mindset, we reflected on the last time we learned something new, we completed a science experiment to calculate our reaction speed (it improved each time), and we listened as she read her personal narrative and gave the most in-depth lesson on the brain I have had since college.

Both of my kids shared how much different it was knowing that they were doing something people would see and experience instead of doing work that gets thrown away. They shared how much more it mattered to complete a meaningful project and display it to teach other people and share what they knew. I shared this on Instagram and got a lot of messages from educators who wanted to know more about how they could do something similar in their school or classroom. I asked my husband, Matt, who has led many exhibitions over the years, for his tips, and he shared the following:

- Embrace the chaos. Most of us like to have things very orderly and controlled, but the learning process is messy.
- Preparation matters. Have all the work completed and prepare students on how and what they will be sharing at the exhibition at least a few days in advance.
- Set the bar high. When kids have high expectations, you will be surprised by what they can and will do.
- Create an environment that feels special. Change the layout, go somewhere, and create an atmosphere and products that are worth sharing.
- A poster isn't a project. Too often, the "project" is something that is done after the learning rather than learning through the project.

When my mom, an amazing retired teacher, attended these exhibitions with us, she reflected: "There is an important difference between exhibitions and the open houses I was in charge of. At these exhibitions, students were involved in the meaningful questions that they cared about, and they were involved in answering them. I saw a passion for the content and excitement in them being able to share what they learned. At my open houses, students were excited to share, but there was no big meaningful question and no long-lasting effect that would make a difference in the community, or world." In a competency-based system, our assessments are a more accurate gauge of what they can do and how they can recall and use knowledge and skills in more authentic contexts as opposed to how well they perform on a test.

Reimagining Parent-Teacher Conferences

I will never forget going to my first parent-teacher conference as a parent instead of a teacher. I was so nervous. My husband and I have collectively led many conferences as the teacher, but sitting on the other side of the table, getting ready to hear about my own kid, was unnerving. We sat down in small plastic chairs, looked at the report card, and went through the numbers: two, three, three, two, four. Multiple worksheets were on hand to provide evidence and validation of the standard and the ranking on the report card.

Matt and I, along with all the other parents, would go through this process twice a year for conferences, yet my kids were never involved at all. They did the work, the teacher graded it, recorded it, and shared it with us at the conference, then I would go home from the conference and share what I understood from their teacher or ask questions, and they would give some vague answer. It was like a game of telephone, where the message gets muffled and jumbled and by the time it gets to the end, it barely resembles the initial intention. Although they may have received a grade, I never really understood where they were in relation to their goals, the learning outcomes, or their peers, and I doubt they did, either.

Year after year, I would leave the conference with a report card and work showing that my kids were getting a mix of twos, threes, and fours, typically on a variety of standards based on multiple tests and assignments but still wondering, "So how are they *really* doing?" What I really wanted to know at the parent-teacher conference had little to do with the percentage of spelling words they got correct, how many math problems they can answer correctly in a minute, or if they accurately copied the words from the board. As a mom and an educator, here is what I wanted at the first conference and still really want to know from my child's teacher.

What is going well?

No matter who you are, start off with celebrations, strengths, or highlights. Call them whatever you want, but please start with what is going well. It is a vulnerable position to get feedback about yourself, let alone your child, and starting with a positive is helpful. I want to know that you see my child and who they are. If I feel like you value them and see who they are and the assets they bring, I will be much more willing to hear the challenges that exist (because they always exist).

How does my child engage with others?

I see my child at home and in settings that I typically have more control over, and I see how my child interacts and reacts, but I have little visibility in the school setting; I only know the snippets that I hear from them when they get home. I want to know what they are like in school. Are they happy? Do they have friends? Do they get along well with others? Are they kind, respectful, courageous? Do they include others or help others? Are there any red flags I should be aware of?

Are they showing growth academically?

It tells me very little if they got a 72 percent on a chapter two test. I really want to know how they are growing in the knowledge, skills, and dispositions that are critical for them to develop as a competent human, like the ability to read and write and communicate their ideas. Can they find relevant information to solve meaningful problems? Do you see progress from your first days with them? What are the goals you are working toward, and how is my child doing? Are they where you would expect them to be? Why or why not?

How can we provide support?

Teachers can feel isolated and too many times, we feel unsupported or even at odds with families. This often comes with miscommunication and assumptions of what each expects of others. If we are clear on what we want the kids to accomplish and where they are in the process, we can all work better together. Overall, as a parent, I want to know how we can work together and what we can do to best support our child's journey. What challenges do you see that we should be aware of? Are there issues we need to understand and address? How can we reinforce and practice what you are working on in school? What might be the next steps?

One of the most reliable ways to get authentic answers to these important questions is for students to lead the conferences themselves. Instead of leaving the kids at home, Matt and I now sit with them and their teachers at a table. In one student-led conference (SLC), Abby welcomed us all, then shared what she was working on in language arts. She then provided a few pieces of her work and an area that she has shown growth in. She did the same for math, science, art, and PE. One of my favorite comments from her was, "One thing I bring to our classroom community is friendship. I feel that I am a good friend and I include everyone." She also noted that although she gets her work done, she can be easily distracted by all of those friends she has. Abby spoke for almost 90 percent of the time. We asked a few questions, and her teacher shared her perspective and the report card that provided further details on the areas Abby covered in the conference. We discussed some data regarding her performance in relation to her grade-level peers, and her teacher shared a few examples about Abby, including how thoughtful and creative she was.

Abby's conference reminded me that although what I hear at the conference is important, what really matters to me is who I hear it from. Listening to Abby share what she was proud of, what was going well, evidence of her growth, and her goals for improving was powerful, and you could see the ownership and preparation had created more purpose and motivated her to own her next steps. When we involve learners and coach them to set goals and track their growth, we allow them to truly own the learning process and empower them to navigate the next steps with confidence.

Portfolio Defense of Learning

I was invited to be a panelist for the eighth graders' portfolio defense at SEEQS Middle School in Hawai'i. The defense is an expected part of the SEEQS experience, where students highlight how they have grown and reflect and capture their learning in a portfolio.

Based on the school's learning philosophy, educators work with students to develop a mastery of core knowledge, skills, and dispositions. In its portfolio-defense guidebook, they highlight:

> The system is divided into two main parts: 1) the portfolio and 2) the defense.
>
> The relationship between the portfolio and the defense is similar to the relationship between a résumé and a job interview. The résumé describes what you can do on paper, and it can be reviewed independently, ahead of time and without you in the room. The job interview, in contrast, is a live event, providing the opportunity for you to expand upon what's in the résumé, and for the interviewer to learn things about you that cannot be communicated on paper.[10]

I was honored to be a part of the process and was amazed at what the students created, how they had captured their learning, and how unique each defense was.

SEEQS has identified five main skills, or competencies, that it wants to develop in young people in order to help create and maintain a sustainable world: reasoning analytically, thinking systemically, collaborating productively, managing effectively, and communicating powerfully. Each student was expected to demonstrate their depth of understanding and application related to these competencies rather than aim for a grade that represented an average of assignments and tests. This allowed for each learner to describe a personalized path to develop and demonstrate mastery through authentic and meaningful learning experiences.

Three different portfolio defenses provided insight into the culture of high expectations and high support. The first student shared his love of video games and how he had grown in his ability to communicate—one of his artifacts was a speech he gave at a climate change rally, and he was featured on the cover of a magazine. This young person was passionate and skilled but had also clearly put his defense together at the last minute. When asked if this was his best work, he acknowledged that it wasn't, and the committee agreed that he did not pass. We gave him kind, specific, and helpful feedback, and he was instructed to work with his advisor to take another shot at his presentation of learning to meet the desired performance criteria.

The second student was articulate and had clearly excelled academically. She had a wide variety of evidence and a beautiful portfolio. The panel agreed that she had clearly developed the skills, but she had failed to use visuals and didn't stick to the time boundary because the presentation wasn't as organized as it could have been. The panel worked through the rubric and expectations and ultimately decided that she should do it again. The reason she didn't pass wasn't because her presentation was not good but because it was not as good as it could have been. We all agreed that she failed to present the best version of herself at this point, and she would develop more confidence and communication skills if she was required to take the feedback, revise, and redo her defense. Her advisor would continue to support her along the way.

The third student shared how she loved to travel and highlighted her growth in the two skills she wanted to focus on. She shared examples from school and how she applied them to her day-to-day life as well as ambitions for the future. It was articulate, personal, and well organized. She met or exceeded all the expectations, and she passed!

It was so fun to be a small part of their journey and see the administration and educators hold kids to high standards while providing clear expectations and models of excellence along with love, support, and guidance to get them there.

Why Measuring What Matters, Matters

I have seen the power of competency-based systems and authentic assessment of learning in learner-centered classrooms and schools. I have also experienced these effective practices in my own defense of my master's degree, which culminated in a presentation, or the portfolio, of work I had curated that aligned to the standards of effective middle-level educators. And as a professor in the same program, I worked with teachers for years to teach, guide, and assess these same competencies to develop and accelerate the practices of amazing educators. This practice has continued for me in my own blog as I continue to capture and share my learning and document my growth in my professional portfolio.

We have an opportunity and obligation to rethink our assessment and accountability practices and use models where learners are developing skills and capturing their learning to show evidence of their mastery, growth over time, and effective learning habits. Instead of focusing on and testing the lowest level of what we want learners to accomplish, let's prioritize the skills that matter most, set high expectations, and allow learners the flexibility, choice, and support to achieve them in a way that is personal and meaningful to them.

Of course, we still have goals and grade-level competencies that we want students to achieve, but learning is not a linear path from one chapter to the next. Real learning that sticks is messy and personal. Instead of focusing on students being behind, let's figure out where they are and acknowledge the jaggedness of their profile. When we put learners at the center and have a clear picture of where they are so they are seen for who they are, then we can support them with the tools and resources to learn, fail, grow, and demonstrate a mastery of concepts instead of just teaching, testing, ranking, and sorting.

As we know, just because we taught something doesn't mean students learned it, but we also have to remember that just because we didn't teach it doesn't mean students didn't learn it, either. As you reflect and read the following chapters about purposeful, personalized, and authentic learning experiences for all students, consider these four questions:

- Are my expectations of students aligned to whole-learner outcomes?
- Do students know what they are expected to learn and be able to do?
- Do I teach them the skills to learn how to learn without me?
- Do I have high expectations and hold them accountable for demonstrating what they learn?

If we shift our focus from teaching to ensuring that learning and a mastery of key knowledge, skills, and habits are at the heart of our work, we can acknowledge where students are and help move them forward. Or more simply, in the words of Hayden, a high school student, "Less assigning, more learning."

PUT IT INTO PRACTICE

Jot down your ideas and share them with your colleagues near and far. **#EvolvingEducation**

QUESTIONS FOR CONSIDERATION

What are the most important outcomes for your learners in your class?

YOUR PLAN:

How might you make the learning targets clear and visible to learners?

YOUR PLAN:

How might learners be able to take ownership of the assessment process?

YOUR PLAN:

PERSONALIZED LEARNING

Learners adapt to the standardized system.	→	*The system adapts to meet the needs of the learner.*

When I was a student, my version of learning how to learn was figuring out that you didn't have to read the whole chapter of the textbook; you could just start with the questions you had been assigned and skim for the answers. I was really proud of myself for figuring that out. Students in Kettle Moraine School District in Wisconsin have a much different experience, thanks to the board change in 2005 that aims to "transform the educational delivery system to better and more efficiently meet the needs of all students." This spurred the district into action, and it continues to push the boundaries of what is possible.

I visited the district's high school and met with students from KM Global, one of the three charter schools that exist within the walls of their legacy high school. All four schools are in the building—one legacy and three charter (KM Global, High School of Health Sciences, and KM Perform)—and they work together to provide personalized options for students. At KM Global, students either occupy one big open room with various spaces to work independently, collaborate in small groups, or meet with their advisor. Each student there also has an adult or learning coach available to guide, support, and monitor their progress, but this teacher is not solely responsible for teaching them.

Students learn through seminars to investigate topics that matter and complete projects based on their interests, goals, and credits needed. This structure empowers students to demonstrate critical thinking and application. Additionally, students take courses that range from direct instruction to technology-enabled courses based on their needs. Students learn beyond the school walls via "job shadows, interviews, field trips, internships, and guest speakers. Students learn firsthand how to communicate and interact with industry professionals and an array of communities and cultures, extending their experience far beyond the traditional classroom."[1] They also have free reign to go to the bathroom, talk to friends, or attend other courses as they please. Essentially, they're treated like humans. Crazy, right?!

Kettle Moraine High School Principal Jeff Walters shared how they are creating a university-based model that meets the needs and interests of the diverse backgrounds, interests, talents, and goals of their student population. Because of this model, teachers continually learn from one another, and students get to opt into smaller, more innovative learning models that have a particular learning focus while still having the opportunity to attend the local high school with sports, electives, and activities like prom, which is a challenge in many small schools. What Kettle Moraine School District has modeled for its community and all educators is that students no longer need to all be doing the same assignments at the same time to learn the same content. Their learning model ensures that "students aren't left behind, nor are they held back, by the rest of their class. We recognize that each child is unique. Each child learns in different ways and at different paces."[2] In a learner-centered paradigm, personalized learning shifts the priority to what is best for the individual rather than what is most comfortable for the system. The following graphic defines the characteristics of the learning model in Kettle Moraine, which ensure that the focus is on learning that meets students' needs rather than programs or curriculum.

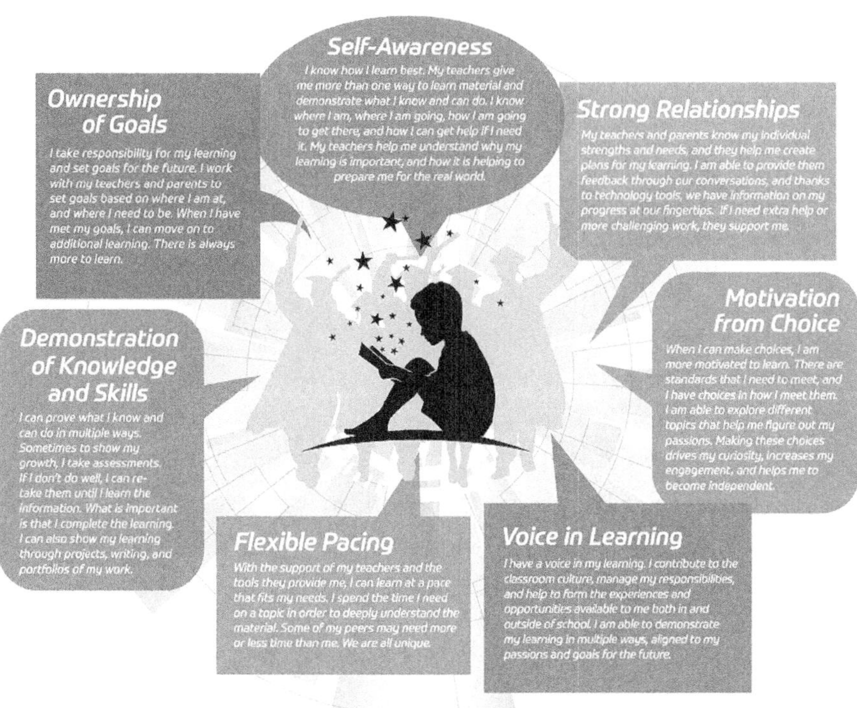

Kettle Moraine Personalized Learning Model

Making the Leap to Personalized Learning

Learners thrive when they have a clear understanding of the vision and know where they are going while still having the autonomy to get there in a way that meets their needs. In an NPR interview, Todd Rose, author of *The End of Average*, describes the emphasis on standardization and its impact on schools and how students learn:

> You think of things like the lockstep, grade-based organization of kids, and you end up sitting in a class for a fixed amount of time and get a one-dimensional rating in the form of a grade, and a one-dimensional standardized assessment. It feels comforting. But if you take the basic idea of jaggedness, if all kids are multidimensional in their talent, their aptitude, you can't reduce them to a single score. It gives us a false sense of precision and gives up on pretending to know anything about these kids.[3]

In spite of our understanding that no two people are the same, we have set up a system that prioritizes and demands overstructured lessons for every student to meet the same objective at the same time in the year regardless of the individual's unique strengths, interests, or questions to be answered.

WHY STANDARDIZE OUR TEACHING WHEN LEARNING IS PERSONAL?

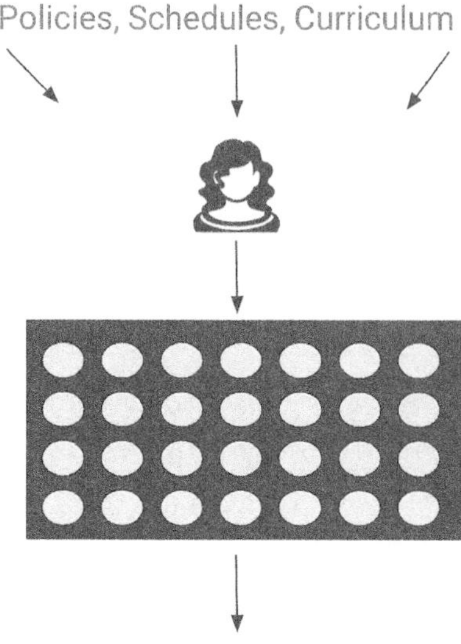

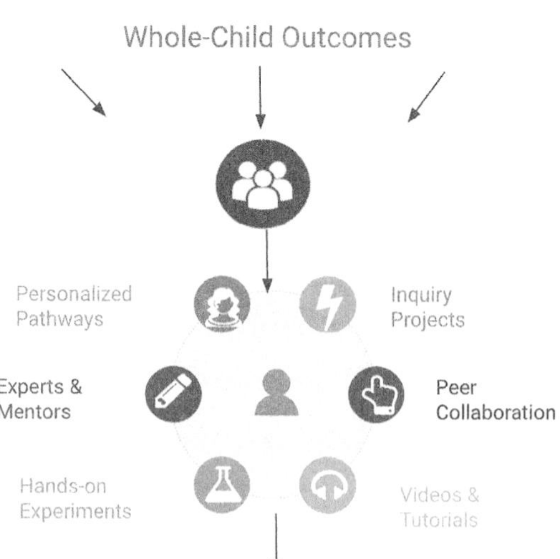

Personalized learning fundamentally shifts the role of the teacher in a school-centered model from one who delivers the content and assesses what has been retained to one in a learner-centered model who sets clear goals, gets to know learners, and adjusts to provide direct instruction while co-constructing meaning or facilitating and coaching learners.

Instruct	Co-construct	Facilitate
• Direct instruction • Mini-lesson • Modeling	• Research and investigate • Identify problems to be solved • Guided inquiry	• Provide feedback • Coaching and guidance • Probing questions

As an instructional coach, I used this model with new teachers and often started co-constructing to guide them through questions and come up with answers to their challenges so they could determine a next step. Depending on their needs and level of expertise, sometimes their challenges would require more instructive methods, such as modeling a lesson or directly teaching a strategy, but I would rarely start here because the learner lacks ownership if I come in as the expert to teach a strategy that may or may not be relevant. On the other end of the spectrum, if I begin with co-constructing goals and planning with a teacher who has ideas they are excited to try, I will switch to facilitator mode, taking on the role of questioner and supporter, as I help put *their* plan into action.

Teachers can use this continuum based on learners' needs to determine when to instruct, co-construct, or facilitate to help identify effective strategies, pinpoint mistakes, and push learners to invent, think, and struggle to grow. A student at Design39Campus, a learner-centered lab school in San Diego, shared her experience as a new student in comparison to her previous school. I love her simple explanation: "At this school, I get to draw it out and estimate and collaborate instead of just doing a string of problems. I feel like I have grown so much from this. Instead of doing a sheet of work by yourself, you work with other people and develop respect for one another." This was a third grader, by the way! When I asked what advice she would give her previous teachers, she said, "Let us work on problems and give us time to figure things out. Try giving less but more complex problems." This advice rings true across all grade levels. Let students try to solve them, share their ideas with their peers, mess up, fix their mistakes, and embrace the struggle and power of perseverance.

What if each student had their own individualized plan?

Individualized education plans that include goal setting have been in place for students with special needs, but if we understand that every child is unique, we have to recognize that all students have strengths, challenges, and special needs. If you are thinking that's impossible, I get it. But consider for a moment how much time is spent designing for the average, meeting the needs of a few, and scaffolding or extending then reteaching. How might the impact shift to create experiences that meet the needs of learners by starting with the learner and providing tools and resources that empower them to navigate varying pathways based on their goals and needs from the start?

One wonderful example of personalized learning is from two co-teachers, Jennifer Tennies and Carole Matson, who co-teach first and second grade in Kettle Moraine School District. In their classroom, students are provided with various models of proficiency so they can identify their current level with respect to the desired goal, set individual goals with the support of their teachers as needed, and work toward them. The following image is an example of the writing models they provided for students, which shows how the students can identify where they are by picking a card to navigate a path based on their current level. This is a first- and second-grade class, and if our youngest students can do this, we can apply these principles across all grade levels.

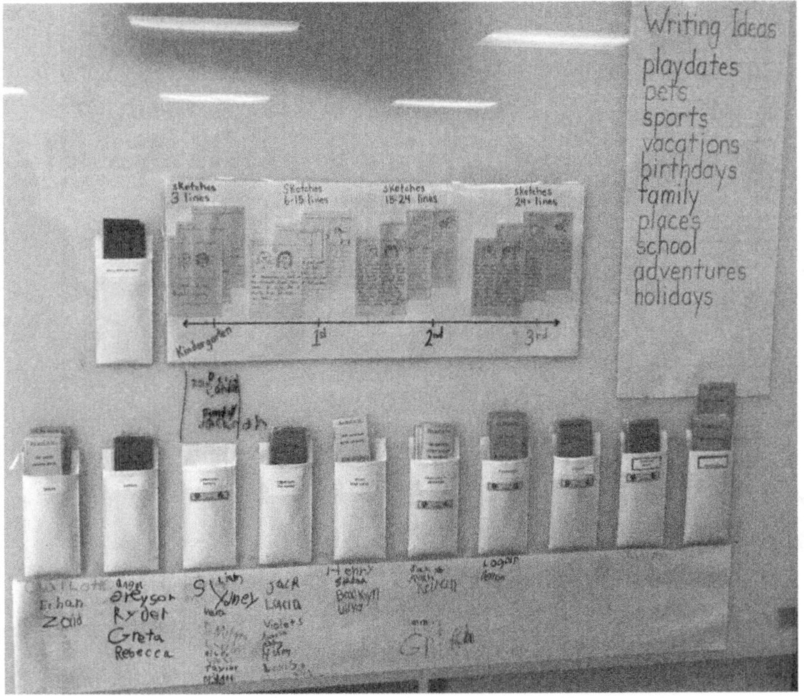

Personalized Learning in Kettle Moraine School District

As has been discussed, learner-centered does not mean "free-for-all." To meet desired learning outcomes, creating a structure that facilitates accountability and progress monitoring will help students stay on track. Here are a few ideas to design more personalized learning experiences.

Must Do, May Do

One strategy that is commonly used is a "Must do, May do" list, where students have certain tasks they have to complete and some choices of tasks they can do if they have time. Some teachers do this on a daily basis, but Kortney Avila, a teacher for Lubbock-Cooper Independent School District (ISD) in Texas, said that she digitally presents students with all the required work and two optional may do activities at the beginning of the week to be due on Friday. This allows for flexibility, as students can work at their own pace and in the order they choose. It alleviates students' stress when they can work on what they choose when they feel it's best for them. During the week, there are options for support and check-ins with small groups. She collaborates with her co-teachers for rotations based on needs, but she said her students' favorite part of the day is when they get to choose what they read because they feel trusted. "Students are excited to hear from other students about books. I'm not at the front of the classroom feeding them books and stories that they have to read, but rather, I let students choose books with their groups. It brought a new excitement to reading for them, and for me, it's been fun to watch. In the spring, we turn our literature circles into podcasts." It's amazing the impact a little choice and trust can have!

Station Rotation

The station rotation model allows students to move in smaller flexible groups to complete a variety of tasks or stations either online or offline. Teachers can set the time and the focus for each station. For example, in an hour, you might be able to start class, connect with students, and get through three fifteen-minute literacy stations that include online/offline independent practice or skill building, partner reading, and small group instruction with the teacher. The teacher can check in with students personally or with an exit ticket at the end of class to see what students learned and determine next steps. This process allows students to work in smaller learning communities and have a sense of ownership and agency over the process, which will often empower them to take their learning above and beyond what we expect from them in a whole group. Many teachers have shared that recording videos for independent work time or mini-lessons has been helpful for students who need to review multiple times and eliminates the need for them to repeat instruction multiple times. Bonus!

Playlists

Although teachers are pretty amazing, as we have seen, with so much information and new content and tools being created each day, it is impossible for anyone to know everything. Depending on the learning goals and the needs of the learners, you can create a playlist of content and resources, like podcasts, YouTube videos, educational content, and so much more. A playlist is basically a collection of resources (created by teachers or students) that students can access digitally with Google Docs or your learning management system to learn the desired content at their own pace, path, and place. You can structure it in a way where all content and activities must be done to complete the playlist, or you may decide to create a playlist with must do and may do activities based on where the learner is and your goals for the learning task. This allows the teacher to work with small groups for direct instruction as needed, provide feedback, and facilitate the learning process at various levels.

Empowering Voice and Choice

We all appreciate the opportunity to make choices rather than being expected to comply. During remote learning, many more teachers began to experiment with more options so their students could make choices about their learning. One example I have enjoyed seeing is teachers posing a complex problem and allowing students to grapple with it, try out various strategies, and share the process of how they solved it instead of simply completing a list of problems. Maybe you could let students choose a book or article they want to read, or have students choose how to respond, either by journaling, using Flipgrid, drawing, or creating a multimedia graphic. You don't have to leave everything open-ended, but consider how students can have a choice in the topic, the resources they choose to learn from, and how they show what they know. Students can also have a choice in the content and how they are learning. Students could have access to podcasts, articles, how-to tutorials, books, experts, a discussion board, or maybe a mix of it all. Choice boards are a great way to organize a limited amount of choices for students and set clear goals with various paths to get there.

Wonder Board

One of my favorite ideas I have seen in a classroom is an "I Wonder" board, where students can post questions they are interested in exploring. Why not host a virtual "I Wonder" board and use Flipgrid or a discussion board to share questions? Students could share what they know or research and comment. If you create a space where kids can engage in topics that are interesting to them and share what they know, they will be much more invested in researching and sharing what they find with others. What problems or challenges do your students see? What are they interested in learning more about?

What I Need (WIN) Time

If you aren't yet ready for station rotations or playlists, there are some small steps you can take to begin making the shift toward personalized learning. Establish a regular What I Need (WIN) time, where students have a block of time to catch up, get support, or investigate something they are curious about. If students need ideas, you can keep a list of questions or topics to investigate during this time and build the skills to learn in small steps.

One of the best ways to figure out how students are doing and what's working is to ask them. In these check-ins, you can connect emotionally and also ask students how they're managing the workload. Ask if students have any feedback on what's working or what can be improved and adjust based on what they share.

Show What You Know

Based on the learning targets and goals, you can find ways to have students share their learning. Anna Rampy, a fourth-grade teacher for Lubbock-Cooper ISD, uses a strategy she calls "This Week in 4th" to wrap up the week and review and set goals. She invites her students to create a video of what they learned in reading, math, science, and social studies and send it to their parents in an effort to reflect on the week. Rampy shared that it is a fun way to see what they remember and how they choose to share their learning. It has also helped her build relationships with her students' families. There is a set time at the end of the week where students can choose videos, pictures, text, or audio to capture their learning and set a goal for the next week. This allows her to quickly assess who was able to understand the content without all the pressure of a grade. She keeps track of their achievements digitally, which gives her great data to pull small groups from. Students then share their data with their parents via Seesaw or Flipgrid, which compiles their work and keeps it as a track record of their learning and growth over time.

Setting Goals

When we set goals, we are more likely to achieve them. Goal setting is a habit that needs to be modeled, practiced, and reflected on to guide students toward building critical skills and developing as skilled learners who can set and achieve their academic, social, and emotional goals. As a middle school teacher, for each project students undertook, I would create or co-create with my students a list of milestones that needed to be completed by specific dates or in a certain progression. We would agree on timelines and create time to reflect on their progress and give and receive feedback to ensure they were on track. This helped them have agency in the process and understand what was expected of them rather than waiting for me to tell them what to do and turn in each day. #GameChanger

This process was really helpful for my students and me. It's important, however, that goal setting is not narrowed down to a mere focus on data and metrics. If personalized learning is reduced to program metrics and advancing to new levels or content without purpose or application, we might achieve our goals but not meaningful results. The purpose of personalized learning and overall learner-centered practices is that students learn how to learn, understand why it matters, and develop the skills to navigate their path beyond school.

James Clear, bestselling author of *Atomic Habits*, teaches us that goals alone are not enough, nor is a narrow focus on the metrics:

> If you completely ignored your goals and focused only on your system, would you still succeed? For example, if you were a basketball coach and you ignored your goal to win a championship and focused only on what your team does at practice each day, would you still get results? I think you would.
>
> The goal in any sport is to finish with the best score, but it would be ridiculous to spend the whole game staring at the scoreboard. The only way to actually win is to get better each day. In the words of three-time Super Bowl winner Bill Walsh, "The score takes care of itself." The same is true for other areas of life. If you want better results, then forget about setting goals. Focus on your system instead.[4]

This is important to remember, as we can get so focused on getting data to show growth and shortsighted metrics of success. That is, we have to be patient and build systems for learners to learn how to learn, and to move forward, we must be mindful of the barriers that exist in learning. It is important to create systems that can ensure students have clear milestones or checkpoints, guidance, and accountability to make progress toward their goals. And remember: it's super important to celebrate growth in learners based on where they are—and it's OK if they aren't where everyone else is. I am a big fan of focusing on what is working, and as the saying goes, when you focus on the good, the good gets better.

Trust and Respect Rather Than Command and Control

The foundation for personalized learning in schools is an environment based on respect and trust rather than control and command. When classroom- or school-based activities nurture young people's emerging sense of self by allowing them to share the responsibility for their learning, they generally thrive. Just as adults enjoy a variety of activities and embrace opportunities for choice, students have varied interests and desires, and they should be afforded the ability to choose, too. There is often room for flexibility in the curriculum where students can use their areas of expertise or interests and still meet content standards. Introducing students to new ideas and opening doors they may not be aware of is a great perk of personalized classrooms. It allows students to build on their strengths while working on areas of growth and pursuing questions and ideas. It helps students investigate issues they care about and allows them to discover new interests. When students are exposed to new ideas and are offered choices, they are motivated to work harder because they will be invested in their learning.

PUT IT INTO PRACTICE

Jot down your ideas and share them with your colleagues near and far. **#EvolvingEducation**

QUESTIONS FOR CONSIDERATION

How might learners have opportunities to navigate their own pace, path, and place?

YOUR PLAN:

How might you intentionally remove barriers for learners to access learning opportunities?

YOUR PLAN:

How might you create a culture of trust and respect?

YOUR PLAN:

EMPOWERING LEARNING

Learners must be compelled to perform.	→	*Learners want to learn.*

Some teachers may fear that making the shift to a learner-centered education will require them to completely overhaul their curriculum—if they even have any wiggle room with their curriculum at all. But my experience at one school showed me that taking an approach that meets the needs of students is not curriculum-dependent. I had the opportunity to visit three classes in a row that were using the same curriculum, and what I saw was vastly different.

Classroom 1: Compliance

I walked into a quiet room with kids sitting in groups of four desks while each student had their own lab instructions and worksheet on their desk. The teacher cold-called students (calling on kids randomly), which is sometimes used as an "engagement" strategy to read the questions aloud. When students were called on, they read with their heads down in a monotone voice, and the teacher repeated the instructions.

One student was directed to add liquid A to liquid C and compare the reaction to the worksheet. Once they assessed the reaction, they called it out for the rest of the class to document on the worksheet. The teacher guided the students step by step through the process.

While they might have covered the curriculum and checked off the standards, the one-size-fits-all lesson likely failed to take students to a deeper level where they may have had a chance to fully comprehend the assignment and represent what they knew in meaningful and authentic ways.

Classroom 2: Engagement

In the second classroom, a few students were joking around with the teacher as we entered and she was conducting a whole-group discussion. She was asking for volunteers to read parts of the instructions, and each group conducted a different part of the experiment and shared their findings. They were engaged, and there was good energy in the classroom, but the class did a lot of the work together. They all completed the worksheets, but the likelihood that each student could do this activity or synthesize the information on their own to make meaning was not evident.

Classroom 3: Agency

In the third class, students worked in pairs and each had the lab instructions. They had to read the directions, set up the experiment, and answer a problem that required them to analyze the results of their findings. Each group had a different mixture, and therefore, their findings would vary and they would have to defend them. Some groups struggled and had to do it a few times, rereading the directions and figuring out why and how the reactions happened. To be honest, I struggled, too, but eventually, I figured it out as I worked with a group through the process.

This classroom showed me that the curriculum might provide the material, but it doesn't have to dictate how we teach. We can teach the content like this teacher did while using strategies that allow students to investigate, problem solve, and shift from being passive learners to owners of the process for more purposeful learning. Regardless of the curriculum, we can create experiences that ignite curiosity, develop passion, and unleash genius. To empower learners to drive their learning, it is critical that we help learners understand that learning is a lifelong pursuit rather than something we do for a test or for the teacher.

Zaretta Hammond, author of *Culturally Responsive Teaching and the Brain*, describes this as the difference between dependent and independent learners.[1] When students are dependent learners, the cognitive load falls on the teachers. To get through the curriculum and stay on pace, we often overscaffold the learning process, especially for learners who we consider to be behind, and often, students fail to develop or use skills to solve problems and engage in the productive struggle that learning requires. An independent learner has strategies, habits, and skills to tackle challenges. They seek resources to solve problems, such as mentors, videos, books, and experiences, and they have the ability to navigate challenges and persevere. Instead of creating systems that demand compliance, what if we instead took the time to model and guide students to develop skills like time management, goal setting, focus, and self-regulation to become the independent, purposeful learners they need to be?

Student Engagement: Are We Focused on Short-Term Results or Long-Term Impact?

Student engagement is paramount in education. If students aren't engaged, they won't invest in the content, attain mastery, and ultimately apply what they've learned, right?

Yet, too often, we focus on engagement in the short term—providing the "shallow fun" of games, enjoyment, and rewards as opposed to believing that students can be engaged through finding deep investment and purpose in their work. We have focused on our fair share of "adrenaline shots" in education. Here are a few common examples:

- When I ask kids what they use their iPads or computers for, I still hear things like "We play games" or "We can go on them when we finish our work" far too often. We continue to think the latest tools and apps are the ticket to engaging our students—they aren't.
- I love a good celebration, and I think we need them, but we have to understand that rewarding a student with pizza for reading books will not inspire lifelong readers any more than putting on a school dance for students who did well on a standardized test will inspire critical thinkers and problem solvers.
- I have seen some of the most beautiful spaces, fully decked out with the latest technology and beautiful, flexible furniture where educators and students play games and build things that are disconnected from any meaningful or relevant learning experiences. Sometimes it's fun, but not always.

Despite our many efforts to reward and engage learners, we know that as students progress through school, they are increasingly disengaged and lack opportunities to build on their unique strengths, talents, and interests.

If we only focus on short-term, extrinsic rewards to coax kids through low-level tasks and provide technology as games or rewards to motivate learners instead of designing authentic and personal learning experiences that draw on their curiosity, passion, and interests, we will not truly engage them. Just as the article "Why the Millions We Spend on Employee Engagement Buys Us So Little" points out that ping-pong tables and other engagement incentives in the workplace don't actually increase employee engagement over time,[2] the newest app or another pizza party might be fun but will fail to increase deeper learning and true engagement if kids are still turning in the same worksheet in order to reap shallow, short-term rewards.

What Does It Mean to Be Engaged?

I participated in a workshop where over five hundred educators were asked how they measured engagement. Many responded that they observe eye contact and whether students nod along, have their cameras on, or answer questions. But these measures equate more to compliance and tell us very little about what students are understanding, thinking, and can do with what they know. If we continue to mistake coming to class, looking at the teacher, and sitting up straight as engagement without creating opportunities for learners to take action and do something that matters to them, we will lose students before we even get started. Worse yet, we will miss the opportunity to help learners set meaningful goals, track their progress, and drive their own learning, which is where true engagement exists.

In a recent research study, Amy Berry, a research fellow at the Australian Council for Educational Research, defined shallow engagement behaviors, such as turning in work, paying attention, and responding to questions, as "participating."[3] She describes these as passive behaviors that have little impact on memory, retention, or learning. Setting goals, seeking feedback, and self-assessment are on the far right of the engagement continuum, where more learning (and joy) happens. This is when students are driving their learning. Yet, according to CASEL, only 52 percent of current high school students report feeling comfortable participating in school and taking risks, even if it means making mistakes. Young people with lower grades from low-income families and those now enrolled in community/vocational postsecondary education are more likely to report holding back in high school for fear of making a mistake. Students often fear speaking up when they don't feel safe or like they don't belong or their ideas aren't valued. It is important that we are sensitive to the factors that may be influencing risk taking and seek ways to remove barriers so all students can engage in deep, purposeful learning.

So how do we improve student engagement? As Daniel Pink shares in *Drive*, "The way that people engage is if they get there under their own steam, and that requires sometimes enormous amounts of autonomy over people's time (when they do what they do), over their technique (how they do it), over their team (who they do it with) and over their task."[4]

Who Is Doing the Work?

There is an increasing trend of parents clearing the path for their children and removing any barriers that could make things more difficult for them—also known as lawnmower parenting. This is typically done with the best intentions, and although I don't love labeling people like this, some of these practices have real implications for how their children develop. In the article "Why 'Lawnmower Parenting' Is Like Robbing Your Kids," Kelley Kitley, a licensed clinical social worker, provides a few examples of how lawnmower parenting can have detrimental effects, such as "pulling strings to get your child onto a certain sports team" or "setting up a rigorous summer schedule that is all work and no play to get ahead." Kitley goes on to say that "if a child fails to complete a homework assignment, a mild lawnmower will say her kid is sick so the child can use the time off school to get the project done."[5] As a parent myself, I acknowledge that it's hard to know the right balance as I, along with many parents, want my children to be successful. Removing barriers can feel like the right thing to do...but is it?

This dilemma happens in the classroom, too. Often out of a desire to help students succeed and remove barriers, teachers end up doing the heavy lifting rather than allowing the students to struggle and learn themselves. James Nottingham describes this struggle as the Learning Pit. More than anything, we need students to understand that struggling is a normal part of learning, not that there is something wrong with them. We also need them to know how to navigate challenges, develop strategies, and push through to emerge with deep learning and the ability to learn again. This is how we improve. There is no way around it.

You might be wondering how we can know when the struggle is no longer productive. Well, it depends. Like Vygotsky described with the zone of proximal development, it varies depending on the learner, the content, and the task. The Pit will look different for different learners. Our job is not to structure each step for each and every learner but to create the culture and checkpoints to help students as they navigate the Learning Pit.

Just to be clear, I am not advocating for abandoning students to figure it out on their own or rely on the support they have—or don't have—at home to help. I believe in the power of teachers, peers, and learning in a community to provide needed support. Giving students the space to struggle only works well if we provide clear learning goals, targeted instruction, support, and collaboration to work through problems and learn new concepts, strategies, and skills. Teachers who provide exposure, guidance, encouragement, checkpoints, and ongoing feedback are critical to the learning process. Teaching learners how to learn and embrace pitfalls to improve can allow students to deepen their engagement and sense of purpose in their learning.

Unpacking the Learning Journey

There are infinite examples of how you can create more opportunities for learner agency in the classroom. Here are a few:

- If you want all students to understand how to identify the main idea without using a basal reader or worksheet from the curriculum, ask students to pick their favorite picture book (at any grade) or an online article and identify the main idea. If your goal is to assess the skill, let them have voice and choice in the process.
- In math, instead of teaching one way to solve a problem and having your students practice it forty times, let them try different strategies on their own (even if they don't end up

working), share their strategies and think with one another, and determine the best way to solve the problem.

- If you are working on argumentative writing, instead of simply assigning a five-paragraph essay, give students a choice on the topic or problems they care about and have them create a video, website, blog, or essay to convey their ideas and construct their argument.
- If you are analyzing an event in history, instead of telling students what happened or reading it from a textbook, provide a variety of articles or primary sources or ask them to do some research and find out what different perspectives exist so they can share what they learned and discuss the event's implications on today's world.

I got to personally experience what purposeful learning looks like a few years ago when Abby came across *Cake Boss* on YouTube. Since she loves sweet things, this exposure to baking experts led her to decide to make some cake pops. She was determined that she knew exactly what to do and gathered ingredients without a recipe and began to "bake." It was a hot mess, which is likely not a surprise to anyone reading this, but to her, it was devastating. She threw the concoction in the trash and proclaimed that she was a failure. She had agency and purpose, but this was not enough to make her dream dessert. She got stuck in the Learning Pit. And because I was busy cleaning up the chocolate mess in my kitchen, I left her there for a while.

Two years later at eleven years old, she proclaimed on the *Today Show* that she "basically taught herself to bake by YouTube." [6] This is an oversimplified (although cute) version of her journey. I want to unpack her learning journey to illustrate how important exposure and purpose, goals and planning, guidance, and revision are to support learner agency so we can empower learners anytime, anywhere.

Exposure and Purpose

Abby's exposure to experts on YouTube and other social media platforms exceeded my knowledge, expertise, and frankly, interest, but because Abby had access to those videos as our learners do today, she could learn anything she wanted. Students can access ideas from experts via a variety of formats, including YouTube tutorials, digital or print books, podcasts, or blogs. They can check out social media accounts and connect with experts in a variety of ways that today's technology has made possible. Abby was consuming content that gave her new ideas and inspired her to create something that was meaningful to her.

Set Goals and Plan

After watching multiple videos, she decided she wanted to make cake pops, which eventually led to cakes and many other desserts and delicious creations. What we both learned from the cake pop fiasco is that a goal is important, but the plan is essential. Once Abby decided what she wanted to try next, before she was allowed to start, she had to show me the plan, prove that she had a recipe, and if she was going to deviate, she needed to know why and have a prediction about what the impact would be. Setting goals is an important part of the learning process and sometimes they are academic, skill-based, or habits we want to create, but being explicit about what you are trying to accomplish and setting a plan helps you accomplish them.

Take Action

The plans only matter if we put them into action and do something. Abby began to regularly try her new ideas and experiment. As much as she gained from YouTube, the real learning happened when she took action and actually tried to make something. With each recipe, she gained new experiences and skills to continually improve. She continues to learn about ingredients and cooking temperatures and make some really great dessert and other dishes. She loves to cook, and we love to test out her creations.

Guidance and Support

A critical part in Abby's journey was my good friend and neighbor, Erica, who took Abby under her wing and mentored her. She would invite her over to help make special cakes and refine her techniques, teaching her when you can and can't deviate from the recipe. She gave her feedback and coached her as she developed new skills. Erica is an excellent baker and an even better human and has provided Abby with invaluable guidance that I could not. I believe that part of our jobs as parents and educators is not only to teach young people what we know, but also to help connect them to others who can support them to learn and grow the skills they need.

Reflect and Revise

As Abby has reflected and revised her techniques through trial and error and with her mentors—both virtual and in-person—she has developed the confidence and competence to take recipes, modify them, and experiment with skill. She now makes time to reflect on what worked when she tries something new or why it was a major fail. Through reflection and revision, we learn and improve and ultimately develop confidence and competence like Abby, who now has taken to live-streaming her cooking lessons with friends and making desserts for me anytime I need to bring something to a party. That's what I call a win-win!

Developing Learner Agency

Exposure + Purpose	Set Goals + Plan	Take Action	Guidance + Support	Reflect + Revise	=	Confidence + Competence
	Set Goals + Plan	Take Action	Guidance + Support	Reflect + Revise	=	Compliance
Exposure + Purpose		Take Action	Guidance + Support	Reflect + Revise	=	Directionless
Exposure + Purpose	Set Goals + Plan		Guidance + Support	Reflect + Revise	=	Stagnant
Exposure + Purpose	Set Goals + Plan	Take Action		Reflect + Revise	=	Slow Growth
Exposure + Purpose	Set Goals + Plan	Take Action	Guidance + Support		=	Plateau

The Power to Act

Agency is, by definition, the power to act, but this doesn't have to be misconstrued as a free-for-all. We all operate within constraints, but we don't have to all do things the same way to reach the intended learning targets and goals. Educators have certain expectations they are accountable for meeting, and there is a variety of content and skills that we want students to learn. Within the content, there can still be opportunities for purposeful learning where learners are engaged and driving their own learning process based on shared goals and expectations.

In order to create opportunities for learners to seek information and learn to learn, here are six questions you could pose to promote learner agency and encourage learners to wonder, explore, and drive their learning (yes, even within your content and standards):

- What do you know, and what do you still need to learn?
- What books, articles, videos, or other resources might help you learn more?
- How does this connect to what you already know?

- What are some creative ways to solve this problem?
- Who are the experts you can learn from?
- How will you share what you are learning?

What if we provided the time and support to engage students in problems that matter and are worth solving to them? How might this change their motivation and perseverance in solving problems and overcoming challenges? What if we provide opportunities that allow students to engage in authentic tasks that foster autonomy, invite the pursuit of mastery, and intrigue them with a sense of purpose? Creating space for learners to answer these questions requires shifting the cognitive load to students and allowing them to embrace the productive struggle.

PUT IT INTO PRACTICE

Jot down your ideas and share them with your colleagues near and far. **#EvolvingEducation**

QUESTIONS FOR CONSIDERATION

How might there be opportunities to create more purposeful learning in your curriculum?

YOUR PLAN:

Are you doing work for students that they could do themselves?

YOUR PLAN:

How might you develop learner agency?

YOUR PLAN:

AUTHENTIC LEARNING

Education is done to the learner.	→	*Education is done by (and with) the learner.*

The year before his unexpected death in 2020, I had the opportunity to meet Sir Ken Robinson and hear his keynote at EDInnovateLive, a conference at the University of San Diego. At one point, he polled the audience and found a few people that spoke three and four languages (so jealous!). As he inquired about how they learned multiple languages, most noted that they were exposed to those languages at an early age. They learned the language through authentically communicating and interacting in context rather than through simply taking classes as I (and probably plenty of the other nonfluent people in the room) had done.

He acknowledged that when children are exposed to different languages early on, they pick them up, not simply because they are linguistically gifted, but because they have an authentic purpose and are exposed to models to learn from. When we are actually curious about something, we develop an authentic urge to learn. It is the curiosity and authentic purpose for learning that propels us to try new things and retain information. The more we are exposed to authentic, real-life settings, the more opportunities we have to learn and grow. This holds true for how we learn many important skills—both academic and social. Curiosity drives intellectual achievement, and those who are more curious about a topic tend to learn faster. Curiosity essentially primes the brain for learning. So, if we want students to learn, it is foundational to spark curiosity in our learners to help them develop the new skills, knowledge, and mindsets we are tasked with teaching them. Otherwise, without curiosity, we might teach, but they may not actually learn.

This point was driven home shortly after the conference as I traveled to the East Coast to visit our family. We went to Niagara Falls, and as we walked along the Falls, the questions just started flowing from Abby and Zack: "Where is the water coming from? Where are the American and Canadian borders? Who decided on the borders? How many gallons per second flow? Can we get ice cream?"

Turns out, I had no idea what the answer was to most of those questions—well, except the ice cream—but we talked about what they thought, read the information provided, then Googled the answers and found out even more. They were so curious about the Falls and the history, which empowered them to ask questions, discuss possibilities, and look up information online. Seeing this interest, I was curious about what a lesson on Niagara Falls might look like.

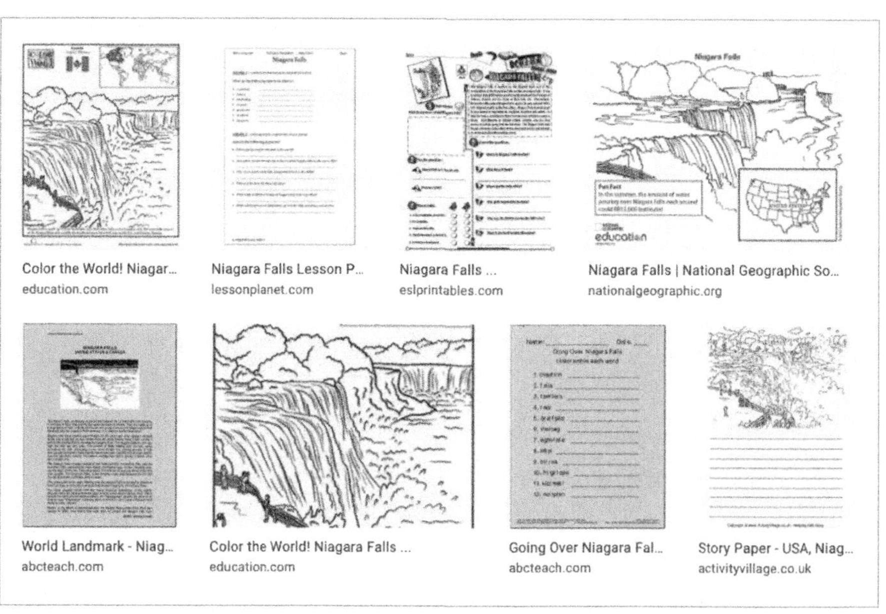

Google Search of Niagara Falls Lesson

To be honest, I can only imagine the groans and lack of interest my kids would have shown if we had given them a worksheet and asked them to find the main idea of a passage or calculate the water flow without the context and their own curiosity to spark questions. They may have done the work out of compliance, but they never would have remembered or cared about any of the information. I also can't help but notice that word scrambles and coloring pages are the majority of the "top lessons." One of the biggest barriers I hear about using more authentic learning is that we don't have time. Cutting out activities or fillers like this would certainly make some room for more authentic learning and be a better use of time.

A few days later, we visited Washington, DC, and visited as many monuments and museums as we could. Visiting a place rich in US history, my kids were again curious and full of questions about past presidents, wars, art, and aviation, and this time, I was struck by how much I had forgotten. I was taken back to the textbooks, unit tests, my utter disdain for history when I was in school, and all the stuff that I had memorized for a test and quickly forgot. It turns out, I am not alone in this. A study in 2014 revealed that first-year college students forget up to 60 percent of the material they learned in high school. Researchers tested nearly six hundred students during their first year at university by giving them fifty minutes to answer thirty-eight multiple choice questions on content they had all learned in high school. The students on average answered 40 percent of the questions correctly. The lead researcher acknowledged, "This is undoubtedly a problem caused by secondary school gearing all of their teachers towards students doing well on exams."[1] Cramming for a test and regurgitating facts is very different from deep, long-term recall and an application of expertise.

It is worth interrogating our curriculum and goals and considering: Where can we go deeper? How can we provide opportunities to go beyond the textbook and explore more stories and authentic experiences of people and the world today? In their book, *Unpack Your Impact*, Naomi O'Brien and LaNesha Tabb highlighted how we recycle the same basic content year after year instead of exploring new ideas and questions and going deeper or expanding our field of study. For example, they wrote, "When we think about people who experienced the horrors of the Holocaust, we are only able to recall one name: Anne Frank. We remember learning about her in fifth grade, eighth grade, and eleventh grade. Anne was important, but we have to wonder—who else and what else can we be teaching about?"[2] They discussed how we learn about Martin Luther King Jr., Harriet Tubman, and Rosa Parks during Black History Month over and over as opposed to learning about the impact of other Black Americans throughout the year.

Authentic learning is about moving beyond the packaged lessons, the sacred units we do year after year, and the single story that is often taught in schools to investigate, think, and learn about the complexities of issues, human lives, and how to investigate and solve problems that matter to us and others. Curiosity is what drives us when we learn about real issues and there is a need to better understand ourselves and the world around us.

Project-Based Learning

How many times have you heard or even said something to the effect of, "We are transforming teaching and learning to meet the demands of the world we live in that continues to evolve at an increasingly rapid pace." As I talk to colleagues and read blogs and research by various thought leaders and practitioners, I notice that the aspirations are more or less the same: we want to create more authentic learning experiences to ensure students develop the skills and mindsets necessary to thrive in a changing world. To meet these goals, many are focused on blended learning, project-based learning, and personal learning. But if you move beyond the labels and talk about instructional practices that promote learning and how they move us toward the desired outcomes for learners, we begin to see that our beliefs and experiences don't always translate to our practices. Many teachers are simply "doing projects" rather than deeply engaging in project-based learning.

Doing a Project	Project-Based Learning
• Comes after the "learning" or at the end of the unit • All projects are the same • The focus is on the product • Turned in to the teacher	• The project *is* the learning • Path and product is driven by learners • The focus is on the process and product • Real-world application and audience

This table highlights the difference between doing a project and engaging in project-based learning. With project-based learning, the project itself is used to teach rigorous academic content and success skills. Students work to answer important questions, such as:

- How can we impact hunger in our community?
- How can we create a more sustainable garden?
- How can we ensure all new members feel included?
- How can we get students to recycle their trash?
- How can we design a more efficient lunch process?

By exploring the question over a couple weeks or longer, students become immersed in it, pursuing answers from various angles. Through this process, they apply what they've learned in meaningful ways. Instruction is incorporated into the project, which is designed to meet appropriate academic goals and standards. The project work creates a genuine need for students to learn grade-level content and skills while working collaboratively, thinking critically, and engaging in reflection and revision.

When educators describe their efforts to "add" authentic learning to their approach, I often hear an initiative-focused approach that sounds like this: "I have to do my thinking maps, AVID strategies, forty-five minutes of 'personalized learning time,' and get through this unit, then I can 'do a PBL.'" But when the focus is on the project or "doing a PBL" rather than what students are learning, we are focused on the wrong aspect of project-based learning. Also, if you do a project and as soon as it is done go back to the worksheets or textbook, we signal that the project was the goal, not necessarily the learning. Instead, if you start with the learners and the learning goals, you can determine which strategies and resources are best to support the learning. With your goals set, you can better prioritize your time to ensure students have opportunities to meet them through authentic and meaningful project-based learning. In a school-centered model, the constant is bells and schedules, and the variable is learning. Why can't we flip that so learning is constant, and the bells, schedules, and resources are in service of learning and learners?

Designing Authentic Projects

As I discussed in chapter 7, many of our students become less engaged in their education the longer they are in school. Much of this is a result of a focus on short-term, extrinsic rewards to coax kids through low-level tasks and provide technology as games or rewards to motivate learners instead of designing authentic and personal learning experiences that draw on their curiosity, passions, and interests. It is important to highlight that if students aren't motivated and inspired to solve authentic and meaningful problems, it's not just them who miss out. It's all of us. In case you haven't been paying attention, we have some very real and challenging problems that we continue to face in our world. If we want to create more engaged, skilled, and empowered learners and citizens, I would argue that we need to create experiences where they can practice and develop these competencies. Consider this example from an article by Education Reimagined, "Why Does Memorization Reign Supreme in Traditional Learning?":

> Imagine a student who aspires to climb Mount Denali—a peak that sits over 20,000 feet above sea level. If his training regimen (i.e. curriculum) only consists of memorizing trail maps, reading memoirs by mountaineers, and climbing the hill near his house, it's clear he would not be developing the skills and stamina needed to successfully complete the journey.[3]

Those who focus on deeper learning not only design experiences that develop skills learners need but help them apply them so they are transferable in every future learning opportunity. When students learn these skills and can apply them, their sense of confidence and preparedness for postsecondary study and life are increased. I like to think of it as a braid weaving together knowledge, skills, and habits with authentic work, which each give purpose to the other.

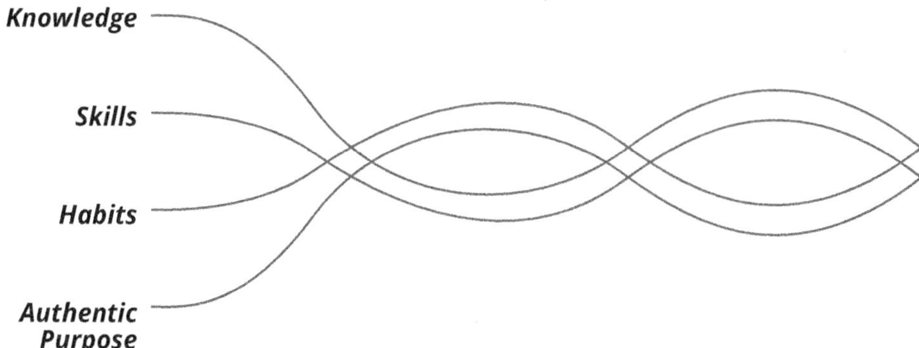

One of the biggest criticisms I hear about a learner-centered approach is that students may have fun but they won't learn the basic skills or key content. However, when you start with a clear end in mind, you can design the projects or any learning experiences to achieve your goals. The following questions and prompts are intended to be addressed sequentially, not all at once.

Overall Goals

- Why does this project matter?
- How does it connect to your learners and their community?
- What successes have you had so far that you want to build on?
- What are some challenges or goals that you have to improve the learning experience?

Success Criteria and Assessment

- What do you want students to learn from this project?
    - What are the academic goals (i.e., knowledge, core content)?
    - What are your goals to practice or learn new skills?
    - What are your goals for habits that students need to develop or practice?
- What does success look like?
- How are you structuring your assignments and tasks to help students meet the success criteria?
- How will you communicate the goals and criteria for success to students?
- How might students self-assess or set goals based on the success criteria?
- When/how might you provide feedback to students based on the success criteria?

Learning Experiences

- What are the key milestones of your project?
- How might these learning experiences provide authentic and relevant experiences that connect to your learners?
- How might students collaborate with peers, experts, or mentors throughout this project?
- How will students learn and develop the skills you will be assessing?
- How might you include opportunities for more voice and choice?
- How might you provide opportunities for sustained inquiry?

Authentic Audience

- How will students share what they know or present their learning in a public forum to demonstrate their learning (i.e., an event, a production, a public product, or a learning exhibition)?
- How might students be engaged in opportunities for critique and revision?
- How will you make student learning and growth visible to others?

As I shared in chapter 2, to create alignment between our vision and goals while maximizing our time and resources, we need to determine what we want students to know, what they should be able to do with what they know, and how we can align our learning experiences to provide the best opportunity to achieve the desired outcomes. Our students know when the work isn't authentic, as exemplified by a comment my son made when I asked him to complete his homework. "Mom, why does it matter? It's just trash can work." He said all his worksheets just went in the trash can anyway, and it made him feel like his work (and he) didn't matter. #Ugh

Investigate Issues That Matter

Every year, current events provide a host of projects to engage in that are relevant and important. These topics, such as the science of infectious disease, exponential growth or spread, economics and the impact of closing businesses, the history of our voting and political system, civic engagement and protesting, the history and implications of racism, global warming and our environment, might pique students' interests; however, they are likely not in the textbook.

To delve deeper, educator Teague Tubach shared in an Edutopia article entitled "Exploring Social Justice Issues Through PBL" that he gave his students a choice about what to research and investigate for their persuasive essay.

> As they learned, they talked. They talked with friends and classmates, with me and their families, and with community members. Some attended protests. What might have been a trivial "What did you learn in school today?" turned into a powerful discourse on injustice and the human condition.

If students need prompts for what to study or investigate, the UN's Sustainable Development Goals provides a framework with seventeen challenges that are relevant to each and every one of us. These goals provide authentic and meaningful topics to learn more about, delve deeper into, and most importantly, take action to make an impact locally and globally. Author, educator, and all-around awesome person Jennifer Williams has launched a worldwide Goals Project where classrooms across the world can sign up to work on a goal together and learn to make an impact.[4] These projects engage learners from kindergarten through high school and model how even our youngest students can make a huge impact. Consider exposing children to these goals and asking them what interests them, what they are wondering, and what ideas they have to take action.

Real-World Learning

During her TEDxKids@ElCajon talk, Rylie Friar, a fifth grader, said that adults often underestimate what kids can do.[5] She cited the example of her business, Rylie's Ruff Toys, which she created at age nine and continues to grow. To prove her point, she highlighted examples of other kids doing amazing work, like Alexa Grabelle, who created the nonprofit Bags of Books, which helps get books in the hands of kids who might not otherwise have access. Alexa has distributed over 120,000 books to schools, homeless shelters, and hospitals.[6] Another thoughtful student, Josh Kaplan, created a nonprofit called GOALS after he noticed that his teammate's sibling couldn't play on their soccer team because of a disability. It is inspiring to see what kids can and will do out of school, and it's even more inspiring to me to see how teachers are creating space and guiding students to learn authentically as they develop their passions, skills, and talents to learn, help, and inspire change.

Sugar Kids Beauty (SKB) is a student-run business where Ashley Greenway and her first-grade students at Elm Street Elementary School in Rome, Georgia, make, sell, market, and learn with their business, making sugar scrubs and bath sprinkles. Students have learned how to operate a business, and they take great pride in crafting their own social media posts, growing their own herbs, and distilling their own essential oils. As they sell their scrubs and other products, they have also learned to calculate profit margins, which total more than thirty thousand dollars and which students have put back into community causes they care about. The business is not a side project that they do in their free time; it's integral to what they learn each day. Students learn about science through the chemistry of making their products, geography as they learn about customers and ship their products, and math through their profits and accounting. They learn about the value of art and design and apply those concepts to their marketing.

John Kopp, a high school teacher in Waynesburg, Pennsylvania, teaches many students with learning differences. These students were often uncomfortable with peers and teachers. In his culinary class, John and his students started Gryphon Student Enterprises, a cutting-board business, with the goal of providing students with the learning community they needed to develop the skills to return to their designated schools and thrive as adults. When the business started, students worked with premade cutting boards and engagement was minimal, but that quickly changed when they began making and designing their own cutting boards. His students not only became more comfortable with each other, but they chose to come to class in their free time to work on their designs for their business.

In the Real World Scholars' 2019–2020 Yearbook, John shared:

> Ethan, a previously reserved student, took to the business and opened up in the process. At a selling event, Ethan took center stage, sharing the business and their cutting boards to a group of 25–30 educators and administrators at a time. The students sold over $300 that day while talking to prospective buyers for advice and feedback on their products. Among them was Executive Director of UI—an administrator overseeing 25 districts in the state—who was surprised by how quickly the students seemed to have outgrown their small town roots.[7]

They not only grew the business, they developed lifelong confidence and skills to succeed far beyond school. So as Rylie suggested, stop underestimating your students and start giving them opportunities to do real, authentic work because she believes kids will surprise you, and so do I!

Profession-Based Learning

One of the key findings in the World Economic Forum's "The Future of Jobs Report 2020" was that the types of skills that are increasingly in demand are problem solving, self-management, effective collaboration, and technology use and development.[8] Corey Mohn, the executive director at Blue Valley Center for Advanced Professional Studies (CAPS), knows that this gap between what we tend to teach in high school and what students need exists, and he works to close this gap with what he calls profession-based learning, where pedagogy, content, and tools focus on preparing students with the necessary skills for life after high school. With profession-based learning, students have opportunities to engage in internships with local business partners, do projects for real clients, and maintain responsibility for a deliverable that clients need. The opportunity to get their first career experience with support and mentoring sets them up with needed skills and a deeper understanding of what drives them personally.

At Blue Valley a student shared the impact of profession-based learning in a video:

> Coming to CAPS has changed my life and my life perspective. I was always pushed to be a doctor, but I always wanted to do something international and help people. Then it came to capstone projects, and I realized I can be a doctor and initiate these projects that will allow me to help others in turn. It opened my mind to the possibility that you don't have to stay on one track. I can really make a change if I want to. Giving high schoolers that freedom of thought to understand this is really important.[9]

When students are involved in real projects that help them gain valuable experience, get to know themselves, and be of service, we can ensure that their time in school is used to deepen their expertise, purpose, and agency and help them chart their course beyond school.

Why Making Learning Public Matters

Ron Berger, CEO of EL Education and an educator, describes how the hierarchy of audience increases engagement and motivation in his co-authored book *Leaders of Their Own Learning*. The lowest levels of engagement come when an assignment is simply assigned and turned in to a teacher. The engagement and motivation increase when there is a more authentic audience such as peers or parents, and it is at its peak when learners have an opportunity to do work that is of true value and can make an impact on the world.[10] I discussed exhibitions in chapter 6, as they are an important part of the assessment process, and it is important to acknowledge here that the public nature of the product and authenticity of the work matter in terms of motivation, purpose, and engagement.

As a parent, there are often plays, concerts, and sporting events where I get to see my children show what they can do talent-wise, yet there are generally few opportunities to see the actual learning my kids are engaged in and watch them demonstrate their skills or share their impact. This changed when we had the opportunity to attend learning exhibitions for our kids, where they performed and shared their work with the community. It is powerful as a mom and an educator to see how an actual event and a public display of their learning motivates learners to take more pride and ownership of their work.

Abby's class worked on a project called Overcoming Obstacles throughout the semester—where much of (but not everything) what they were reading, writing, discussing, and creating tied into this theme. The kids had been learning about challenges—physical, mental, and emotional—and worked over the semester to train for a team triathlon, where one student paddleboarded (instead of swimming), another biked, and another ran. In addition to training for each of the events, they read and wrote biographies about people who had overcome challenges and the lessons they learned. They wrote poems about their strengths, and their poems were published along with pictures that represented each of their unique talents. They also wrote and produced a song and made a video that they sent to *The Ellen DeGeneres Show*—the prospect of Ellen noticing their work was motivation enough!

It was at the final exhibition that the students had the chance to share what they'd learned with an authentic audience—their families, teachers, and hopefully Ellen. An authentic audience pushes learners to work hard and go through the process to create the best product because their work is made public. My daughter and the other fourth graders in her school convened at the beach for the triathlon. Cheered on by her classmates, families, and other teachers, Abby had to get on a bike and work through some obstacles to complete the triathlon in front of hundreds of people. If it had not been for the public forum, she likely would have quit.

Each of these opportunities to present to an authentic audience took the basic skills and standards she was learning and put them in a context that mattered. Not only did she learn and improve in her reading, speaking, writing, and communicating, but she also demonstrated these skills in ways that were authentic and meaningful to her. The best part for me, as her mom, was watching her struggle and grow as a person in each of these experiences.

Here are a few examples:

- She forgot her bike on the day of the triathlon and had to borrow one that didn't quite fit (or work), but she had to jump on the bike and do her best (we both agreed she needs improvement in responsibility but showed great character in her resilience and perseverance). She was frustrated and wanted to quit, but there was an authentic audience, and she persevered and made it. That lesson is worth its weight in gold!
- When she was supposed to get up and recite her poem, the printer broke, and she wanted to quit. She was nervous and wanted to blame other people, but the show was starting and she pulled herself together, got up there, and read her poem. We were all proud of her accomplishment.
- She wrote a rap and practiced with her classmates over and over until they got it right and had developed her writing (and rapping) skills while also in the process developing strong friendships, which means the world to her—and us.

Author Thomas Friedman reminds us that "the world doesn't care about what you know. It only cares about what you do with what you know." Authentic learning is often at odds with the need to cover, document, and assess. The standards we teach are important, but when we connect them to the students' lives and experiences and help them expand their worldview, we teach and they learn so much more.

It Doesn't Have to Be All or Nothing

Incorporating all of the elements of authentic learning all the time can be overwhelming or downright unsustainable based on each teacher's context and learner needs. I love how Kristyn Kamps, a PBL educator and coach, advocates for a "dimmer switch" approach:

> With the "dimmer switch" approach, teachers use many (not all) project design elements in their unit plans. They can continue to highlight and use those elements outside project work to keep the language and mindset of PBL alive, even when students are not engaged in Gold Standard project work. The more elements that are in use, the higher the dimmer switch setting and the "brighter" the PBL experience becomes. Some units are more PBL-esque, and some units are less, but the PBL approach never goes completely dark.[11]

The project (much like any curriculum) is important, but it isn't the end goal. It is the vehicle that allows learners to develop the skills, knowledge, and mindsets needed to engage as productive learners, workers, and citizens. Learning comes about through cycles of action and reflection—where students encounter, tinker, choose, practice, and contribute to new experiences, then describe, evaluate, connect, envision, and integrate to make meaning of those experiences. Students learn to engage in authentic problem solving that will allow them to be active and contributing members of society now and in the future.

PUT IT INTO PRACTICE

Jot down your ideas and share them with your colleagues near and far. **#EvolvingEducation**

QUESTIONS FOR CONSIDERATION

How might you provide the time and support to engage your students in solving problems that matter to them?

YOUR PLAN:

How might students have opportunities to develop and explore new questions?

YOUR PLAN:

How might their new skills and knowledge be embedded and developed through authentic projects and problem solving?

YOUR PLAN:

How might students have opportunities to engage in real-world learning?

YOUR PLAN:

PART III

HOW MIGHT WE CREATE THE ENABLING CONDITIONS TO SHIFT TO A LEARNER- CENTERED PARADIGM?

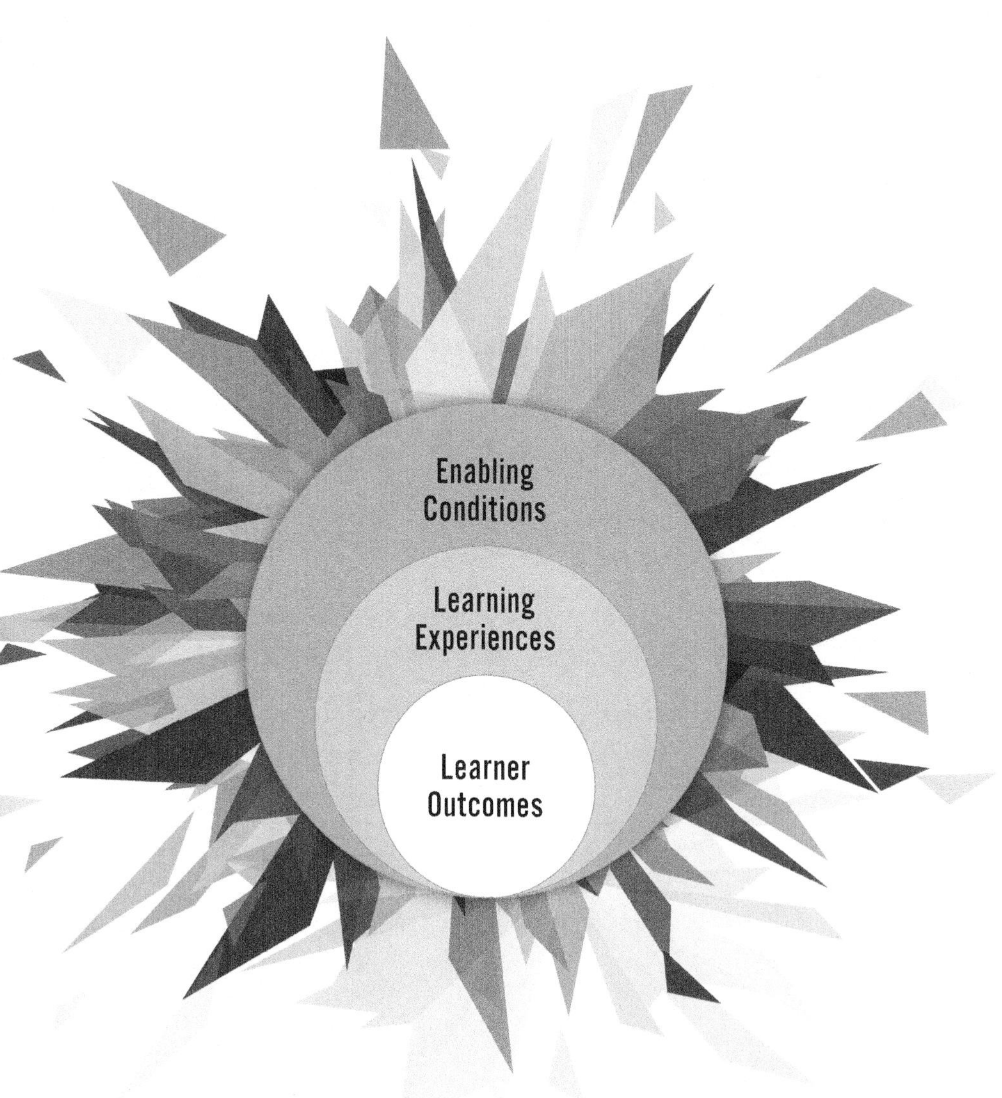

While the first section delved into how we see learners and the second focused on key practices, the final section will focus on how we can shift our mindset. In part III, we will look at the third circle of the learner-centered ecosystem to create the enabling conditions for meaningful change. This section begins with examples of human-centered design to consider how we can create the conditions for learner-centered experiences. In chapter 11, we will explore examples and practical tips to navigate change, and finally, in chapter 12, we will discuss why and how we must challenge the status quo to shift to a learner-centered paradigm.

In chapters 10 through 12, these key shifts will be addressed.

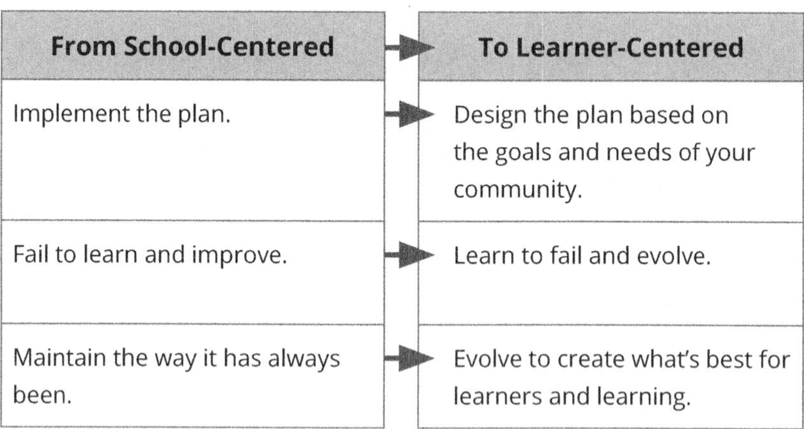

From School-Centered		To Learner-Centered
Implement the plan.	→	Design the plan based on the goals and needs of your community.
Fail to learn and improve.	→	Learn to fail and evolve.
Maintain the way it has always been.	→	Evolve to create what's best for learners and learning.

DESIGN THE FUTURE

Implement the plan.	→	*Design the plan based on the goals and needs of your community.*

As I have mentioned throughout this book, our aspirations and goals are not always aligned with our practices. Now is the time to address this misalignment head-on and be intentional about the design of our learning experiences and environment moving forward. The future of education will require new school models, new approaches for teaching and learning, and innovative leaders in and out of the classroom who can create the conditions for meaningful change. Throughout the book, we have explored the essential components of learner-centered education. Now, to turn this into action, you will need to empathize, ideate, prototype, and design learning experiences that will accelerate the shift to effective and empowering learning experiences for all of your students. As Steve Jobs said, "The best way to predict the future is to invent it."

Sara Blakely, the founder of SPANX, a shapewear company with the mission of improving the lives of women, created her products and company because no other product lived up to her expectations. In fact, she said that every product she tried caused some kind of discomfort or just didn't work as she imagined it could or should. She needed something better, but she also knew that many other women did, too. So, instead of designing something that worked for her as she prototyped her own products, she obsessively focused on her customers and getting a variety of feedback from diverse women to design and make products that worked for those she aimed to serve. She didn't just want to create what worked for her; she was intent on creating something her customers really wanted and valued. Her customer focus has been one of the main keys to her success, and that's what makes her products top of the line and her strategy one that many have begun to emulate.

Her idea began with her own experience, but she knew that, to create something that worked for all kinds of women and now men, she needed to empathize with others, prototype, and get feedback from real people with different perspectives and body types to make sure her product met their needs, not just hers. So, you might be wondering why I am telling you about SPANX in a book about education. I am glad you asked. I believe Sara's orientation is one we can learn from as we look to design the future of education. I believe it is important to look for and learn from models all around us in and out of education to truly expand our view of what is possible. A popular phrase among educators is "Be the teacher you wish you had." I disagree. If we are learner-centered, it's not about the classroom or the strategies that work for us or that we wanted years ago. Our experiences can give us empathy, but evolving education is about the learners you serve and designing the learning experiences for *their* context. It's not about being the teacher you needed. It's about being the teacher *they* need.

To that end, we have to acknowledge that our educational systems, like bell schedules, curriculum, pacing, space, and grades, were designed by people, and they can be redesigned or switched out for new ones by people like you. Here are some questions that can spark ideas for a system redesign. You might have other ideas. Please add them to the list and share them with others.

- How might we design a system where each learner gets what they need?
- How might we invent new structures and systems that are more just and inclusive?
- How might we create more flexible schedules and spaces for learners?
- How might we collaborate to build on the strengths of our educators and community organizations instead of working in isolation?
- How might we redesign our assessment or grading practices?
- How might we teach our children the skills, knowledge, and habits that will equip them to listen, collaborate, and solve problems that matter now and in their future?

Human-Centered Design

I often work with teams of educators to think of students whose needs are not met in school—their most marginalized students—and dig deep to understand their needs in order to better design for them. To do this, we must start with human-centered design. There are many different design-thinking frameworks and experienced designers will tell you that although a framework is helpful, applying the framework in real life rarely results in a linear process. Instead, we can go back and forth many times between various steps and points. I prefer to use the Liberatory Design framework created by Stanford's K–12 d.school and the National Equity Project. On the National Equity Project website, they share, "The Liberatory Design is both a flexible process that can be used by teams and a set of equity leadership habits that can be practiced daily."

Noticing is crucial to understanding your power, bias, and actions within the context you exist in. Closely connected to noticing is empathizing with those you are designing for to truly see the problem from multiple perspectives. Once you have seen the problem from multiple perspectives, you can define it and begin to generate ideas to solve the problem. Then once many ideas have been explored, designers can prototype and test their ideas to get them out into the world to get feedback and improve them. The goal is to get it right through iteration instead of waiting until you think it is right before you share. Reflection is crucial throughout the process, as is noticing the context and checking your biases and beliefs.

As I have worked with educators to design a day, a week, or an entirely new model, we always find ways to more effectively meet the needs of diverse populations. Many of these ideas and examples I have shared with you in this book. Different groups identify various archetypes of students "at the margins," who a typical school rarely meets the needs of. We start by discussing specific students, not general patterns or averages, and empathize with what they feel and think while reflecting on what they do and say to give us insight. Creating an empathy map can help think about students as individuals rather than generalizing the population as a whole. Empathy maps highlight students for whom the pace of school is moving too slow, students who are behind because school is moving too fast and they can't catch up, students who primarily speak a different language and need different access and opportunities to learn the content and skills, and students with social-emotional needs who are overstimulated and prefer fewer interactions with people but still want to be connected. When you consider the impact on students on the margins who aren't always successful with a school-centered model, we can design new and better ways to meet the needs of each and every learner. Like Sara Blakely did with SPANX, with this framing we, too, can be obsessively focused on learners and their needs and design variations that will help them meet their goals.

Here is an example of how you can use design thinking to create a more learner-centered approach.

NOTICE: Pick students you currently work with who are struggling, such as students who are disengaged because they aren't being challenged, students who are struggling socially and emotionally, and students who aren't motivated and seem to check out. Take time to notice and reflect on what is working and what isn't. Think about which students are successful in your school or classes and why. Examine your role, biases, beliefs, and impact.

EMPATHIZE: By empathizing with students and what they are experiencing, you can identify what students are saying, thinking, doing (or not), and feeling. This exercise will allow you to better consider what circumstances students are dealing with so you can think about and design a better system that would support them as an individual instead of trying to fit each one of these students into a preexisting system. To gather insight about how to better design lessons and empathize with learners, you can do empathy interviews with students. Conduct thirty-minute interviews, and ask questions like:

- What is school like for you?
- Do you feel valued? By whom?
- When do you feel successful inside the classroom?
- When have you felt unsuccessful?
- How might you improve this school?

DEFINE: The next step in the process is to define a need, which can be done with a simple sentence frame: **who** needs **what** because **why**? Here are some examples of what might come up:

- Students need clear goals and pathways because they are overwhelmed.
- Students need smaller class sizes and fewer interactions because they become easily overstimulated.
- Students need more opportunities to apply learning through authentic projects and exploring passions to be challenged at an appropriate level.

IDEATE: Based on these problem statements, think about how you can address these challenges. Ideation is a central strategy in design thinking, and as Linus Pauling said, "The best way to have a good idea is to have a lot of ideas." To generate a lot of ideas, we must spend time ideating with a "yes and" stance, which builds on ideas instead of shutting them down. This helps everyone share as many ideas as possible to allow students to be more successful and create new and better opportunities for them to learn and reach their full potential. The goal should not necessarily be to have the best idea but to think about generating a lot of ideas to create new and better systems to evolve what currently exists.

PROTOTYPE: Once all of the ideas are on the table, teams can start to design a new strategy for a day or week in the life of their students. Think about what structures you can redesign by answering the following questions:

- What are the desired skills, knowledge, and dispositions for students to learn?
- How will students learn?
- Where will students learn?
- When will students learn?
- Who will support their learning journey?
- How will students track their progress and work toward mastery?

Although students' needs will vary, you can design more learner-centered experiences by starting with the learners—who they are and what they need, clear learning goals and priorities, pathways for each learner, and flexible learning environments.

TEST: This process can be done to reimagine an assignment for a student, a whole class, or even a new model for your school or district. The goal is to do something and test out your ideas. Start small and keep testing as you learn and see the impact. The smallest steps can lead to the biggest impact, but you will never know unless you try.

REFLECT: Margaret Wheatley reminds us that, "Without reflection, we go blindly on our way, creating more unintended consequences and failing to achieve anything useful." Even with the best of intentions, we can miss the mark if we don't stop and pause to reflect. This was made clear to me as I talked to a teacher who had just been in a three-hour workshop learning a lot of new content. He shared, "I really like these ideas, and I'm totally invested, but after three hours of new information, I am so overwhelmed." Then he stopped and wondered aloud, "Is this what our students feel like?" Too often, the answer is yes!

If we just keep adding more content without taking the time to process what fits together, what can be taken out, what is repetitive, what is missing, and what "it" means, we will burn out teachers and students and fail to have the impact we want to have. Teachers, just like all learners, need time to process and make sense of all the new initiatives and mandates to figure out how to best implement them in their classrooms with their students.

The "right" answers to the previous questions will vary based on the context and learners. But I have no doubt that caring and talented educators can create new and better opportunities to meet the needs of those in their schools and classrooms by reframing challenges and considering multiple perspectives. Author and educator A.J. Juliani pointed out on his website that, "Our job as parents, teachers, and leaders is not to prepare kids for something; our job is to help kids prepare themselves for anything."[1] If we use this goal as a starting point, reframing the problems we face can help us design novel solutions. This doesn't mean we are starting from scratch. As we evolve in education, we look to our learners, build on what works, and leave behind practices that no longer serve our communities to better meet the needs of learners in a continually changing world.

The Constant Is the Learning; the Variables Are the Location, Time, and Place

When we begin with what we want for learners and design from there, we can create new and better learner-centered models. Change can be daunting if we think about the system at large and focus on everything that is wrong. You don't have to transform the system as a whole to make an impact; you can simply start with your class, an assignment, the schedule, or your beliefs. These incremental changes are essential to shifting the system as a whole. Start small, make tweaks, and assess the impact. As you learn and make mistakes, you will grow and keep evolving to meet the needs of your learners and create models for others of what is possible. It just takes one step to lead to others. Mary Davenport, a high school English teacher, detailed her shift in approach to reduce the amount of content and homework she assigned in order for students to pause and reflect on their learning and maximize learning. She was forced to rethink her priorities: "As someone who has mastered the curriculum mapping style of get it done to move on to get that next thing done, using an approach of slow down and reduce has been quite a shift for me. However, the shift has been necessary. What matters most is what's best for my students, as opposed to my own plans or mandates imposed by others."[2]

Casey Rimmer, who leads professional learning for public schools in Union County, North Carolina, created quickly designed online courses for teachers who couldn't meet in person. She found that teachers benefitted from access to asynchronous modules, but they were missing connection and collaboration. To get the best of both worlds, she created a weekly opportunity for teachers to share what they were learning and highlight what was working. Some joined live, while others watched the videos later at their own convenience. She reimagined the use of time and space to allow teachers to learn in more personal and flexible ways that met their needs.

Educators have come up with mentoring programs and varied schedules and have set up regular check-ins with students, created outdoor schools or learning environments, and redesigned lessons and grading policies. They have leveraged technology to connect, document, and communicate what has been learned. More connections have been made with community partners and global experts through virtual connections. These are just a few of the ideas and actions that have come out of noticing a need, reflecting on the possibilities, and designing new and better solutions for learners and learning.

COVID-19 caused many of us educators to evolve to meet the needs of those we serve. There is no doubt that it has transformed how we learn and interact with one another. For many of us, making these shifts illustrated that creating lasting change in how we teach is about more than learning about the latest technology or digitizing learning experiences. Adding more content, more assignments, and more meetings will not enable us to create something better if we don't prioritize and focus on what matters most. The steps you take can have a lasting impact on your students and community. As Mother Teresa acknowledged, "I alone cannot change the world, but I can cast a stone across the waters to create many ripples." Our school-centered systems are well established, and the shift to learner-centered systems won't happen overnight. But the evolution of educational practices is happening in classrooms all across the world because of educators who understand their learners and design new and better systems each day in their classrooms and schools. These incremental shifts compound day over day. Big changes begin with small steps.

PUT IT INTO PRACTICE

Jot down your ideas and share them with your colleagues near and far. **#EvolvingEducation**

QUESTIONS FOR CONSIDERATION

How might you use human-centered design in your context?

YOUR PLAN:

What challenges or inequities do you notice?

YOUR PLAN:

How might you empathize with students or other community stakeholders to better understand their needs?

YOUR PLAN:

What ideas would you like to test?

YOUR PLAN:

What is stopping you from moving forward?

YOUR PLAN:

CHAPTER 11

NAVIGATE CHANGE

Fail to learn and improve. → *Learn to fail and evolve.*

A teacher shared a story with me of an innovative plan for a class to do passion-based projects they had spent months working on as a team. But when they finally implemented them, things didn't go exactly as planned. They considered it a failure, promptly scrapped it, and "went back to normal." Things not going according to plan is not failure; it's real life. We don't learn and make an impact by creating the perfect plan. We learn by testing our ideas, finding out what works, and getting feedback to improve. Still, things being imperfect is the crux of so much fear and what keeps the status quo prevailing. This fear of failure is common among educators. Here are some things that many of us (myself included) are afraid of:

- Not knowing how things will turn out
- A chaotic learning environment or a lesson that doesn't go according to plan
- Students struggling

- Being judged by your peers, parents, admin, students, etc.
- Not getting through the curriculum
- Students not being "prepared" for the next grade
- Not having all the answers
- Not being enough

The list goes on and on. I get it. These are real concerns. There is no guarantee that everything will go according to plan, and our lessons and plans "fail" regularly whether we admit it or not. What is perfect for one student may not meet the needs of another, and what worked on Monday doesn't always work on Tuesday. When I lead professional learning sessions, teach graduate classes, and work with districts on implementation plans, things don't always go exactly as I had planned, but that doesn't mean I've failed. If you are open to adaptation and stay true to your goal and purpose rather than sticking to your plan at all costs, you'll have a great opportunity to learn, understand better, and move forward.

The potential cost of failure feels far riskier and more damaging than managing the status quo. But as I think about what I want for my kids and all young people, I have been thinking a lot about what it means to fail. The more I think about this, the more I realize that failure, to me, is that zip codes can predict test scores, more than half a million students drop out every year, the tutoring industry outside of the school day is a gold mine, and student engagement and motivation decline rapidly the longer they are in school. Failure is that more kids are ill-prepared for the workforce, young people are increasingly underemployed and plain lost, and high-stakes standardized accountability systems so often are at odds with authentic learning, identity development, and belonging. Failure is the revolving door of teachers leaving the profession because they don't have enough support, resources, or trust to do their jobs and they don't feel like they can fulfill their why with the conditions they find themselves in. Failing on a lesson plan or a new strategy is part of the learning process, and it's OK. Failing to step out of your comfort zone and change practices to better meet the needs of students is not. If we were really afraid of failing our students and our communities, we would be relentless about looking to the learners we serve to evolve our pedagogical practices. This also requires creating systems and policies that support a more holistic view of success that aligns school to the world we live in and getting rid of the ones that impede authentic learning, growth, and innovation.

The Beginner's Mindset

When we look at failure as part of the process in our evolution, we can move from a deficit mindset and embrace the vulnerability that gives birth to our creativity and innovation. Learning new processes, procedures, and tools can be hard when you are used to being an expert, but it can also provide you with a fresh perspective on how to avoid going back to normal and instead design a better way forward. The concept of a beginner's mind comes from Zen Buddhism and is called *shoshin*, or "having an attitude of openness, eagerness, and lack of preconceptions when studying a subject, even when studying at an advanced level, just as a beginner in that subject would."[1]

When something is new, there is no expectation to know anything about it. This allows you to approach the situation with a different mindset than one of an expert, who has a preconceived notion of what should happen. This can put you on autopilot rather than helping you think about new and different opportunities.

A beginner is:

- Open to how things work and new possibilities
- Free of expectations about what will happen
- Curious and wants to understand things more deeply

And as Brené Brown reminds us, "There is no innovation (or love, or joy, or growth) without vulnerability." Those who are willing to show up and be brave, not perfect, are paving the way and innovating to create the path forward.

(Dis)obedience

In her book *Untamed*, *New York Times* best-selling author Glennon Doyle shared one anecdote that really stood out to me as an educator. She writes about how when she married her wife, she didn't allow her mom to visit because of the fear she was harboring about her family opinions, and she wouldn't let her bring that fear to her children. She reminds us that no matter the love and respect you have for your parents, "A woman becomes a responsible parent when she stops being an obedient daughter."

Just for a refresher, here is what *obedience* means: "compliance with an order, request, or law or submission to another's authority."[2]

This resonates with me, as I can recall my mom telling me as a young girl that she made sure that phrase about being an obedient wife was taken out of the wedding vows between her and my dad. As a strong woman and teacher, my mom has always modeled respect, love, and impact over obedience as a parent and an educator.

Reading this passage about obedience made me reflect about my experience as a teacher and all the many expectations and rules we're given to follow. I was once told the reason that teachers get a discount on car insurance is because they are more compliant and don't often take risks. Many of us tend to trust the administration or the "authority," which can be the department head or more experienced teachers, and just follow the rules to avoid getting into trouble.

While I believe that administrators and people in the district and state departments have good intentions, they don't know your kids and their circumstances, nor do they have knowledge of what your day-to-day is like as an educator. Simple obedience will never create the experiences our students need, nor will it allow us to make the changes we need to get us to the outcomes we desire. If we want students to be able to navigate their own path and have the skills and confidence to make choices, shouldn't we model that as teachers?

What if we reframed this statement and said, "A teacher becomes a responsible educator when they stop being an obedient employee." Gasp, I know!

Hear me out—the best educators I know have always looked to their learners and used their professional expertise to make decisions. Isn't this the goal? I am not saying that we do whatever we want without regard to the rules and regulations; that never goes well. But I am encouraging educators at all levels to not just blindly follow the rules because someone with more authority or seniority made them. A learner-centered paradigm of change is where we start with what's best for the students, then work outward to create the conditions to empower them. This stands in contrast to the "outside in" theory of change that begins with policy makers then goes to districts then schools then teachers and finally students, which hasn't worked for far too many. The way we have always done things is not the way forward. Many rules and systems were designed for a different era and should rightfully be interrogated and challenged. Going against the grain can be scary and hard, but it can also allow us to try new things and ditch some practices that were ineffective.

While too many teachers see the administrators as a barrier, I have never had one superintendent or principal tell me how proud they were of a teacher for following the rules or take me to visit a classroom because the teacher was on track with the pacing guide. They often showcase the teachers who are creative, empowering learners, and willing to take risks. When we let obedience and perceived barriers get in the way instead of just having conversations about what is the best way forward, we miss out on opportunities to have a tremendous impact. As one teacher shared with me, "There is nothing worse than teaching something in the pacing guide when you know there is a better way to teach it." I would argue that there is something worse: not doing what you know to be right for your students. If you know there is a better way to meet the needs of learners, you owe it to them (and yourself) to try it. And when you do, we will all be better for it if you bring others with you by sharing your thinking and what you learn..

Let It Go, Let It Goooo . . .

If you are now singing the song from *Frozen*, so am I. Elsa, the ice queen, exemplifies how letting go is what is needed for change. All change starts with an ending and letting go, which is very difficult for us as humans to do. This might explain why we hold on to the binders for each new initiative or try to fit in everything we would do in a typical day, even when we have students learning from their bedrooms and we are teaching from the kitchen counter.

Grief counselor William Bridges has studied how people grieve and manage transitions, and they are very similar. In his book, *Managing Transitions*, he highlights three stages of change: 1) endings, 2) neutral zone, and 3) new beginnings.[3] As you evolve as an educator and shift practices, it is normal to go through these phases, and naming them and the emotions you feel can be helpful to let go, navigate the neutral zone, and embrace new beginnings as you manage changes in your own career.

Stage 1. Endings

Moving from school-centered to learner-centered practices, even if it aligns with your personal vision, can be hard because it requires letting go of practices that are comfortable and putting an end to the way things have always been done. This could be deciding to get rid of your seating chart, not doing the butterfly unit and giving students a choice of topics to study, or changing your grading policy. This causes uncertainty, frustration, confusion, and anger but also excitement toward a new path forward.

Stage 2. Neutral Zone

This is an opportunity for innovation and creativity, where you are imagining, planning, and unsure of what exactly will be the new normal. This is a phase of navigating between skepticism and exploration, which can cause anxiety but is also where you can dream about what is possible after you have decided to let the old way go. You might consider how students will decide where to sit, what the expectations will be, and how you will organize learning experiences where students have choice but are still able to meet learning goals. You might explore how you can assess what students have learned without a final exam or averaging all their grades for a final grade.

Stage 3. New Beginnings

New beginnings are a time of high energy—consider the beginning of every school year. Teachers go through these stages every year, saying goodbye to one class and welcoming a new one. We can do this with our practices, too. This doesn't mean we weren't good enough in previous years or that our practices were ineffective; it means we can decide to let go of what no longer aligns with our vision and desired goals and create new and better experiences. There is often a feeling of accomplishment when you see students sitting in various seats or pods collaborating and meaningfully engaging in learning experiences that are based on their choices and interests. There's joy when students are able to show evidence that they have mastered the competencies connected to the defined learning goals or when your new grading system accurately reflects the evidence of what they know and can do and not just what has been completed (or not).

It's not the change that we are often opposed to; it is the transition process that is daunting. The loss of identity and the way of the life or teaching that is comfortable, the lack of clarity in the neutral zone, and the risk of failing in a new beginning.

Like any type of learning, managing change is not a linear, step-by-step process. You will go back and forth through the zones, and you may feel many emotions at the same time. Naming the process and identifying where you are can help you collaborate with others to navigate the transitions more openly and creatively.

I believe we can change the world through the type of education and access we provide for all children. This begins with being honest about what we need to let go of, understanding what is possible, and working together to navigate the change process. And to get better and continue to evolve, we need to be opening doors, asking questions, and sharing concerns about our education systems that many have in private but rarely share in public. Elementary teacher Justin Minkel pushes us to realize that, too often, we are not nearly as brave in the classroom as we expect our students to be, and it's holding us all back. Instead, he shares, "I dare us all to stop worrying about looking good to our principal, to parents, to visitors from the school board. I dare us to try instead to actually become good for the children in our care."[4]

PUT IT INTO PRACTICE

Jot down your ideas and share them with your colleagues near and far. **#EvolvingEducation**

QUESTIONS FOR CONSIDERATION

What does failure mean to you?

YOUR PLAN:

How might you prioritize what's best for learners?

YOUR PLAN:

How might you use the neutral zone and new beginnings to make space for creativity and innovation?

YOUR PLAN:

What can you let go of?

YOUR PLAN:

CHALLENGE THE STATUS QUO

Maintain the way it has always been.	→	*Evolve to create what's best for learners and learning.*

In 1999, the US women's soccer team wanted to play in the NFL stadiums like the men's teams. FIFA, the sport's governing association, said no. Women's teams had not traditionally made enough money, and the belief was that they would never sell enough tickets to make it profitable. Despite the lack of support and vision from the top, the US women's national soccer team set out to accomplish what no one thought possible. According to Abby Wambach, previous US women's team captain and author of *Wolfpack*, "They were united and committed to a vision that they knew was possible and determined to bring to life." They worked together to make their vision a reality and challenged the status quo, and eventually they got to play at the Rose Bowl Stadium in Pasadena at a game attended by ninety thousand people, the largest crowd ever to attend a women's sporting event. Wambach shares, "There were suddenly new rules to the game—written by those women—but only because a bunch of badass visionaries had the courage to break the old ones."[1] I remember reading this in an arcade while

I waited for my kids and their friends to spend all their money and found myself crying over some nachos. Now, I love soccer, but my tears were not necessarily about the sport; they were about the courage of these women and those who followed them to challenge the status quo and redefine the rules.

I feel the same way when I walk into schools and see educators who have had the courage to stand up and challenge the status quo to create what kids today not only need but deserve. It's also because I know the status quo is strong and alive in many aspects of our lives and fighting for something new and different is not always easy. I also know that without challenging norms and fighting for what you believe, you will never get to experience something better.

The status quo makes it easy to sort and rank.

The status quo maintains hierarchy.

The status quo feels safe.

When you are so used to a compliance-driven model, it is often hard to imagine that kids (and all people) can function outside of a control and command environment because we are so used to how people operate in our existing systems. When I bring educators to visit the schools I have shared with you throughout this book, they are always struck by the culture of care and agency rather than control. High school students have meetings off campus, connect with mentors, and work on projects in hospitals and boardrooms. Students are using tools, building houses, writing code, and starting movements in their communities and beyond. Early elementary school kids are allowed to choose seats, get a drink of water, and even move freely in and out of the classroom. Kids are celebrated and coached to make good choices and are not scolded, trained, and managed. When you see a student eating, listening to music, or talking to a friend, it doesn't have to be an affront to the teacher or a challenge to authority. It's just kids being human. The focus is on learning and what people need, not a dress code, infractions, and educators being in control. And when kids feel trusted, they don't test the rules as much because they don't need to. It is so clear that they feel valued and empowered, and frankly, they get to spend more time on learning, which is the goal!

How Do I Get "the Other Teachers" on Board?

Building the momentum that creates change is always easier and more fun with others. It is hard to be the lone duck seeking change, so it is no surprise that when I am facilitating professional learning days or a conference workshop, one of the questions I get asked most often is, "How do I get the other teachers on board?" If you are reading this, chances are you have been or are ready to shift practices to create more learner-centered experiences and environments, but I know you might be wondering how to move other people forward so all kids in your school or district have similar opportunities.

I feel an incredible sense of urgency, and I know many of you do, too, but it is important to remember that in pursuit of growth and evolution, when we label people as resistant to change, veterans, stuck in their ways, etc., we isolate people and create more barriers to the change we want to see. Remember from the previous chapter, it's often not the change that people are opposed to, it's the transition, and you can help them navigate it.

New innovations and ideas are great, but if you can't encourage people to use them in ways that can improve lives, it won't matter. As Melinda Gates writes in *The Moment of Lift*:

> Their cup is not empty; you can't just pour your ideas into it. Their cup is already full, so you have to understand what is in their cup. If you don't understand the meaning and beliefs behind a community of practice, you won't present your ideas in the context of their values and concerns, and people won't hear you.[2]

We must keep that in mind if we're looking to change the practices or behaviors of others. If we really want to move people forward (this includes students, colleagues, families, and administrators), first we have to see them and know them, then we can grow them.

Here are some ways to work with others to move forward:

1. Focus on People, Not Programs

When I lead professional learning or work with anybody, I begin with who they are and where they are. If I ever forget this, I am quickly reminded that any change requires the individual to take action, and they have to want to take steps forward. Often, the focus on technology or innovation rather than learning further alienates those who are hesitant to experiment with new practices. To encourage meaningful change in education, we have to first understand and communicate how any new change will create opportunities for powerful learning. As Simon Sinek encourages in his powerful TED talk, "How Great Leaders Inspire Action," "Start with why."[3] If not, we run the risk of burning out teachers by adding more and more to their plates without a clear understanding of why these new approaches are important. We will also continue to waste lots of time and money on new programs and tools if we don't help teachers understand the demand for a paradigm shift in education, along with the possibilities of how our current technology aligned with learner-centered pedagogy can and should impact their classrooms.

2. Celebrate What's Working

The educational system is inherently deficit-based. Too often, we focus on what is wrong with someone and how to fix them rather than starting with what is working well. Instead, when we seek out ways to celebrate others and show what is working, we validate people and can build off of their strengths.

What I was reminded of reading *The Moment of Lift* is that behaviors are hard to change, and in education, just like all other human endeavors, it's not about the program; it's the delivery method that matters. To shift practices, we need to be clear about our goals and why they matter, understand and honor people's beliefs, provide opportunities for connection, learning, and new experiences, and ensure that we celebrate what is working. The reality is you can't make other people change, but you can create the conditions and provide examples to inspire and encourage people to shift their practices and work together toward a common goal.

As I have worked with different groups of educators, from teachers to administrators, I have started to be more intentional about starting off with celebrations. I often start with, "Tell me something good," which is what I say to my own kids regularly. I love the song by Rufus and Chaka Khan, but the message and impact are even more important. It is easy to focus on what is not working and pinpoint all the things that are wrong as opposed to what is going well or even simple steps in the right direction. Usually people turn to a partner and freeze because they aren't used to focusing on something that is going well, or they just revert back to a challenge. But knowing the benefit, I push each person to focus on some success, growth, or positive moment, and with that, the momentum usually shifts and people start to smile and engage differently.

I know I am not always the best at this, and it's helpful for me to create structures and habits that can help me celebrate the good in myself and others. Here are three simple ways to create routines that help you and others celebrate the good.

Begin a staff meeting or morning circle with celebrations. Take fifteen minutes to highlight what you notice in others, focus on what is going well, build each other up, and intentionally create rituals that ensure individuals feel seen, valued, and inspired to make an impact. Our students have a lot going on, and just like adults, it's easy for them to focus on what's not working or what they didn't do right, but if you can start your days or even once a week with a celebration and allow students to verbally share something they notice about each other, it can shift the course of someone's whole day.

Create a space for shout-outs. There's a good bit of research that suggests your happiness increases when you show gratitude. In our office, we have a wall and a virtual space for people to shout out one another and acknowledge when someone has a big win or did something that made a difference for others. Teachers deserve these shout-outs almost every minute of the day and don't get them nearly enough. Make time to acknowledge the incredible work that happens in your school or community. It's powerful for those being recognized as well as those who are celebrating their colleagues.

Intentionally look for the good. I love to work with educators and plan for their aspirations and what we really want school to be, but it can also be overwhelming to think about so many things that need to shift. As you continue to grow and evolve, it is critical that you make time to walk through classrooms with the lens of what's working. When you meet with students or colleagues, try to identify and highlight progress, growth, and positives and let them know what you see.

There is so much that happens throughout the week, and it is easy to get bogged down by the challenges, but it makes such a difference when we focus on the positives and celebrate one another because when we focus on the good, the good gets better. This is not to say that we should ignore challenges and only focus on the good, but it does mean we should create time and space to acknowledge and celebrate success.

People are more confident and passionate and do better work when you focus on what's right with them instead of what's wrong with them. Creating authentic learning experiences that empower people to develop the skills and talents to manage themselves and build on their assets, rather than focus on their deficits, maximizes the motivation, contribution, and impact of all learners.

3. Connect to the Heart

I sat with a principal as I was working with his team, and we talked about his goals and what he wanted to see on his campus related to the larger district vision. He started talking about programs and specific expectations that were all very status quo and typical. As he continued talking, his tone shifted and he passionately shared, "I just want to see kids working in groups. I just want to see authentic collaboration and work happening in classrooms!"

His demeanor changed, and he started to open up and get real; he started to tell his story. He started reflecting on his own experiences and shared the resistance that he, too, had as a teacher and how he thought that kids wouldn't pay attention and that they weren't going to listen and it wouldn't work in his class. Yet, in spite of all of his fears, he tried anyway and found out that he was way more successful and way happier as a teacher and spent the last three-fourths of his teaching career helping kids collaborate and work together. You could see his passion. We were all leaning in and moved by his openness and vulnerability.

Then he stopped, turned to the group, and genuinely asked, "How do I get my teachers to understand this? How do I get my teachers to see this?"

"Have you shared your story?" I asked.

"Can it be that simple?" he questioned.

He had never even thought about sharing his story, his passion, and what he really wanted to see in classrooms. Instead, he had shared the district vision, talked about the programs, and walked through classrooms to check on progress. He had gone through the motions and had seen some shifts, but he wanted more, and my hunch was that his teachers wanted more from him, too.

To be clear, I don't think it's as simple as telling your story, but it's a good place to start. It is critical that we connect with those we serve about why this work matters to us. To inspire others, we can start by sharing our own experiences, strengths, challenges, and fears. Also, in telling his story and reflecting on his experience, this principal was reminded of his own fears as a teacher and the long process he had gone through to change his practices. He began to empathize a bit more with the struggles his teachers were facing.

Your stories matter because they're part of who you are.

Your stories matter because they provide a window into how you see the world.

Your stories matter because they help you build relationships and connect on a personal level.

Telling your stories as a leader can help open up space for others to tell their stories and for us all to learn from the experiences of others. Too often, we can get caught up in the programs, policies, and procedures, but it is the relationships we foster and a culture of learning and growth that create the conditions for meaningful change. Stories help us do that.

George Couros wrote about the ten characteristics of a twenty-first-century educator, and when I first read it, I pushed back on the idea that everyone had to be a "storyteller." But in true George fashion, he helped me see the power in telling our stories, and I have really come to understand why storytelling is an essential characteristic for all educators. He says:

> If we want meaningful change, we have to make a connection to the heart before we make a connection to the mind. People have to feel something. Simply sharing information is not a way to create this connection, but we have to think about how we create this connection. Telling stories helps people create their own connections and meaning, and in a world that is information rich, we are vying for the attention of our students. These stories we tell are the ones that stick with our students (and colleagues) longer than simply sharing ideas. We need to share information in different ways that are memorable and compelling. Your story and stories matter, and will resonate long after our time with our students.[4]

You might not feel you have anything meaningful to share, but we all have a story to tell. The best educators don't tell others what to do; they inspire people by their stories and actions, model the way, and support individuals along the path to continuously move forward.

4. Find Your People

As my husband, Matt, was finishing his tenth year of teaching, he had become frustrated by the mandates and bureaucratic systems, a frustration that was compounded by the lack of resources and support. He was unhappy and not as effective as he wanted to be. He had become part of an ineffective system, moving groups of uninspired and disconnected kids through school, and it was weighing him down. As he was contemplating whether or not he should leave education, he took a chance, branched out of his comfort zone, and moved schools. Within that first month at his new school, I saw him transform as an educator in such powerful ways. He was working harder than I had ever seen him work, visiting families of students, asking tons of questions, seeking feedback on new ideas, collaborating with his colleagues, designing projects, enthusiastically connecting with students in and out of class, and overall loving his job. He started in a pilot program with Real World Scholars with his tenth-grade chemistry students.[5] Since then, they have made and sold lots of soap, improved and expanded their products, and provided scholarships for fellow students with their proceeds. His class has been featured by Google, and his school was recently recognized as one of the "14 Most Innovative Schools in America."[6]

I highlight these accomplishments not only because I am proud of what he and his students have done, but more so to acknowledge that you, too, are capable of all you dream of. Marie Forleo, entrepreneur and best-selling author of *Everything is Figureoutable*, says, "You wouldn't have the dream in your heart if you didn't have what it takes to make it happen." Remember, you are enough, you are capable, and it's time to take that step to create what you want.

I am not necessarily advocating you go find another school, but what I am acknowledging is that we are influenced by those we surround ourselves with. If you aren't inspired and motivated by those closest to you, find people who lift you up and who you can lift up as well. There is nothing more motivating than working toward a common purpose with like-minded friends and colleagues who are equally passionate and fill you up. It doesn't just give us meaning and fulfillment; it inspires us to keep going.

It is easy to become isolated in our roles as educators and overwhelmed by the enormous pace of change in the world and education. I have found that connecting with those who lift you up and push you to be better is well worth the investment. In his book *Crossing the Unknown Seas*, David Whyte sums up the power of a community that builds up one another so work can be taken on with purpose and joy: "You know that the antidote to exhaustion is not necessarily rest? The antidote to exhaustion is wholeheartedness."[7]

Educators are busy with life and work, and, no doubt, their plates are full. But when we connect with others to engage, learn, and grow, we can be filled with a sense of "wholeheartedness." To continuously move forward, it is critical to have people push you and affirm your path. There is too much work to be done, and the stakes are too high to go at it alone.

5. Share Your Ideas

Dave Burgess, former teacher, author, and CEO of Dave Burgess Consulting, Inc., has created a publishing company and a community that has inspired educators all over the world to connect, share, and learn from each other. I have benefitted from being a part of this community and made some great friends in the process. We have all learned a lot from Dave, but his push to share ideas is unfortunately contrary to how many educators think and how school cultures operate. This analogy he uses is important: "Imagine you were at a party and knew CPR and didn't save someone because you were afraid of bragging or showing off your talents. You wouldn't do that. You would run over and save the person's life." So as a teacher, he believes (and I agree) it is your moral obligation to share your ideas with others. Your ideas, experiences, and lessons learned could change the way students all over the world learn. If you share and someone else takes those ideas and builds on them, your impact has grown exponentially. Students get to learn in new and better ways because you shared with their teacher. Being great doesn't mean you are trying to be better than others; it means you are trying to be the best for your students. It is not a zero-sum game. Instead, we know that we rise by lifting others, and when we attack each other or keep our ideas tucked away in our classrooms, we all lose.

Being great doesn't mean you are trying to be better than others; it means you are trying to be the best for your students.

6. Be the Good

I have worked with educators around the world in small rural communities, on islands in the Pacific, in the middle of Alaska, in urban cities, in suburban communities, and across charter, public, and private schools. At a superficial level, there seem to be so many differences, and sure, there are many differences in the food, culture, dialect, and geography, but at the core, I always find that, as people, we have so much more in common than the differences we tend to focus on. Regardless of where I ask people about their aspirations for learners, the responses are the same: We all want kids to be healthy, happy, confident, capable learners and problem solvers. We want kids who can understand multiple perspectives, read and make sense of the mass amount of information, and communicate their ideas effectively. We won't be able to do this for kids if we don't expect it of ourselves and model this for them.

My favorite quote from Buddha that I have on my wall says, "Believe there is good in the world," with emphasis on "Be the Good." This inspires me every day to look for and celebrate the good, and it reminds me that I have to first expect this of myself before I expect it in others. If we really want to create learning environments in our schools where all learners are valued and seen as capable of achieving desired outcomes, we have to begin with the belief that they can.

When we celebrate and honor the differences in one another, including culture, race, gender, experiences, and preferences as assets that people bring with them, we can create a more interesting, inclusive, and welcoming learning community and world. Our differences are strengths, not deficits.

As a teacher, every time I tried something new with my students, I learned very quickly what worked and what didn't. As an instructional coach, I had the opportunity to work with other teachers to help them shift practices to better teach and impact how and what students were learning. To this day, every time I walk into a school or a classroom, I see and learn new things and better understand the barriers we face, but most of all, I continue to expand my view of what is possible, as I see so many examples in diverse schools who are leading the way.

In *Good to Great*, Jim Collins says, "Greatness is not a function of circumstance. Greatness, it turns out, is largely a matter of conscious choice and discipline."[8] We have a choice in schools today to maintain the status quo or look at what we want for our students, communities, and our collective future. To get where we want to be will require us to decide to do better and challenge the status quo to get there.

Small Shifts Lead to Big Changes

Visiting thousands of classrooms across the world not only validated my practices, but it also provided me with insight into the tremendous shifts in education. It's inspiring to see educators who are looking to their learners, creating empowering learning experiences based on their needs, and creating the conditions to move forward. I have also noticed the discrepancy in the range of access and opportunities kids have in schools. As I am encouraged to see more and more learner-centered practices, I also feel a sense of urgency to make these experiences and environments the norm for the education of all young people and the adults that teach them.

I am optimistic as I continue to see positive shifts that point toward progress in our education system and challenge the status quo to create new and better opportunities for learners across the world. I would be remiss, however, if I didn't acknowledge that I know there is a wide range of access and opportunities that learners have. Although at times it can feel daunting to think about the enormous challenges of shifting entire systems, whether it be in the classroom, a school, a district, or the whole nation, I know it is possible and it is so important to look at the progress we continue to make. Keep sharing, connecting, and pushing each other to evolve and meet the needs of the learners in your classrooms today and tomorrow.

I have grown exponentially in my professional life in the past years because I have been more open about my ideas and have connected with educators around the world who have pushed and expanded my thinking about what is possible in our schools today. As I continue to learn and evolve, I know I have to model the same practices that I hope to see other educators model and practice in their classrooms. I have to be open to learning from success and failure. To be perfectly honest, I still struggle every time I teach a class, lead professional learning, or share new ideas, and I often wonder if my ideas will resonate or if the experiences I have designed are the right ones. It takes courage to show up and be vulnerable, and I constantly channel Brené Brown, who says, "Vulnerability is the birthplace of innovation, creativity and change."[9] Because I have experienced the benefit and know how it has helped me improve and grow, I continue to put myself out there and test my ideas. I have created this book to share these ideas with you in hopes that they will spark an idea and inspire you to see what is possible.

Remember, it's the small changes, one step at a time, that build, and together, we can create big shifts that open doors and create opportunities for all learners. Let's do this!

PUT IT INTO PRACTICE

Jot down your ideas and share them with your colleagues near and far. **#EvolvingEducation**

QUESTIONS FOR CONSIDERATION

Why might it be important to challenge the status quo?

YOUR PLAN:

How might you get others on board?

YOUR PLAN:

What sparks can you set in motion right now?

YOUR PLAN:

INTRODUCTION

1 Oscar Wilde, *The Picture of Dorian Gray* (London: Wordsworth Classics, 1992).

2 Education Reimagined, "A Transformational Vision for Education in the US," education-reimagined.org/wp-content/uploads/2021/01/A-Transformational-Vision-for-Education-in-the-US.pdf.

CHAPTER 1

1 Sir Ken Robinson, "Do Schools Kill Creativity?" filmed February 2006 in Monterey, CA, TED video, ted.com/talks/sir_ken_robinson_do_schools_kill_creativity.

2 Ibid.

CHAPTER 2

1 Pam Leo, "Connecting Through Filling the Love Cup," The Natural Child Project, last modified 2007, naturalchild.org/articles/pam_leo/love_cup.html.

2 C. Kirabo Jackson, Shanette C. Porter, John Q. Easton, Alyssa Blanchard, and Sebastián Kiguel, "School Effects on Socio-Emotional Development, School-Based Arrests, and Educational Attainment," NBER Working Paper No. 26759, February 2020, nber.org/system/files/working_papers/w26759/w26759.pdf.

3 Marc Brackett, *Permission to Feel* (London: Quercus Publishing, 2019).

4 Marc Brackett, "Feelings Influence Decisions," last modified November 10, 2019, marcbrackett.com/feelings-influence-decisions/.

5 "Boost Emotional Intelligence with the Mood Meter," Heart-Mind Online, last modified September 2014, heartmindonline.org/resources/boost-emotional-intelligence-with-the-mood-meter.

6 Amy Fast, @fastcrayon, Twitter, January 2021, 6:48 p.m., twitter.com/fastcrayon/status/1347359373815734273?s=20.

7 Julia Freeland Fisher and Daniel Fisher, *Who You Know: Unlocking Innovations that Expand Students' Networks* (New York: Wiley, 2018).

8 World of Work, worldofwork.net.

9 Nepris Career Explorer, nepris.com/misc/careersearch.

CHAPTER 3

1 Julie Henry, "Teacher Bias Gives Better Marks to Favourite Pupils, Research Reveals," *Telegraph*, last modified January 6, 2013, telegraph.co.uk/news/9782323/Teacher-bias-gives-better-marks-to-favourite-pupils-research-reveals.html.

2 Nicholas Papageorge and Seth Gershenson, "Do Teacher Expectations Matter?" Brookings, last modified September 16, 2016, brookings.edu/blog/brown-center-chalkboard/2016/09/16/do-teacher-expectations-matter.

3 Alix Spiegel, "Teachers' Expectations Can Influence How Students Perform," NPR, last modified September 17, 2012, npr.org/sections/health-shots/2012/09/18/161159263/teachers-expectations-can-influence-how-students-perform.

4 Daniel Coyle, "The Simple Phrase That Increases Effort 40%," last modified December 13, 2013, danielcoyle.com/2013/12/13/the-simple-phrase-that-increases-effort-40.

CHAPTER 4

1 Mandy Froehlich, "I'm Not Your Ideal Graduate," last modified February 17, 2020, mandyfroehlich.com/2020/02/17/im-not-your-ideal-graduate.

2 Laura McBain and Lisa Kay Solomon, "Educator as Futurist: Moving Beyond 'Preparing for the Future' to 'Shaping the Future,'" Medium, last modified October 2, 2020, medium.com/@laura_11350.

3 Brené Brown, *Daring Greatly: How the Courage to Be Vulnerable Transforms the Way We Live, Love, Parent, and Lead* (New York: Avery, 2015 reprint).

4 Collaborative for Academic, Social, and Emotional Learning (CASEL), casel.org.

5 Populace Research, populace.org/research.

6 Justin Reich and Jal Mehta, "Imagining September: Principles and Design Elements for Ambitious Schools during COVID-19," EdArXiv, last modified July 3, 2020, edarxiv.org/gqa2w.

7 Linda S. Gottfredson, "Circumscription and Compromise: A Developmental Theory of Occupational Aspirations," *Journal of Counseling Psychology Monograph* 28, no. 6 (November 1981), www1.udel.edu/educ/gottfredson/reprints/1981CCtheory.pdf.

8 Sarah Lewis, *The Rise: Creativity, the Gift of Failure, and the Search for Mastery* (New York: Simon & Schuster, 2014).

CHAPTER 5

1 "Introduction to the Learning Sciences," Digital Promise, researchmap.digitalpromise.org/topics/introduction-learning-sciences.

2 EUSD Farm Lab, Facebook page, facebook.com/EUSD-Farm-Lab-1404838366405369.

3 Youki Terada, "New Research Makes a Powerful Case for PBL," Edutopia, February 21, 2021, edutopia.org/article/new-research-makes-powerful-case-pbl.

CHAPTER 6

1 Heather C. Hill, "Does Studying Student Data Really Raise Test Scores?" *EducationWeek*, last modified February 7, 2020, edweek.org/technology/opinion-does-studying-student-data-really-raise-test-scores/2020/02.

2 Rick Stiggins, Judith Arter, Jan Chappuis, and Steve Chappuis, *Classroom Assessment for Student Learning: Doing It Right, Using It Well* (London: Pearson Education, 2004).

3 Joe Feldman, *Grading for Equity: What It Is, Why It Matters, and How It Can Transform Schools and Classrooms* (Thousand Oaks, CA: Corwin, 2018).

4 Betheny Gross, Sivan Tuchman, and Susan Patrick, "A National Landscape Scan of Personalized Learning in K–12 Education in the United States," iNACOL, last modified June 2018, aurora-institute.org/resource/a-national-landscape-scan-of-personalized-learning-in-k-12-education-in-the-united-states.

5 Lindsay Unified School District, *Beyond Reform: Systemic Shifts Toward Personalized Learning* (Bloomington, IN: Marzano Research, 2017).

6 Education Reimagined, "A Transformational Vison for Education in the US".

7 Thomas Guskey, *Get Set, Go!: Creating Successful Grading and Reporting Systems* (Bloomington, IN: Solution Tree Press, 2020).

8 Rachel Lawsum, Twitter, October 7, 2020, 8:25 a.m., twitter.com/rlawsum/status/1313848027912704000.

9 Share Your Learning, shareyourlearning.org.

10 "Why SEEQS?" SEEQS, seeqs.org/why-seeqs.

CHAPTER 7

1. "About KM Global," KM Global, kmsd.edu/domain/821.
2. "Personalized Learning in Kettle Moraine," Kettle Moraine School District, kmsd.edu/domain/468.
3. Anya Kamenetz, "Standards, Grades, and Tests Are Wildly Outdated, Argues 'End of Average,'" last modified February 16, 2016, npr.org/sections/ed/2016/02/16/465753501/standards-grades-and-tests-are-wildly-outdated-argues-end-of-average.
4. James Clear, *Atomic Habits: An Easy & Proven Way to Build Good Habits & Break Bad Ones* (New York: Avery, 2018).

CHAPTER 8

1. Zaretta Hammond, *Culturally Responsive Teaching and the Brain: Promoting Authentic Engagement and Rigor among Culturally and Linguistically Diverse Students* (Thousand Oaks, CA: Corwin, 2014).
2. Jacob Morgan, "Why the Millions We Spend on Employee Engagement Buys Us So Little," *Harvard Business Review*, last modified March 10, 2017, hbr.org/2017/03/why-the-millions-we-spend-on-employee-engagement-buy-us-so-little.
3. Amy Berry, "Disrupting to Driving: Exploring Upper Elementary School Teachers' Perspectives on Student Engagement," *Teachers and Teaching* 26, no. 2 (2020).
4. Daniel Pink, *Drive: The Surprising Truth About What Motivates People* (New York City: Riverhead Books, 2009).
5. Nicole Spector, "Why 'Lawnmower Parenting' Is Like Robbing Your Kids—And How to Actually Help Them," last modified March 27, 2019, nbcnews.com/better/lifestyle/why-lawnmower-parenting-robbing-your-kids-how-actually-help-them-ncna987526.
6. "How 2 Different Families Are Approaching Kids and Tech," *Today* video, 3:28, from segment aired on August 7, 2019, today.com/video/how-2-different-families-are-approaching-kids-and-tech-65494597512.

CHAPTER 9

1. Jaleesa Baulkman, "First-Year College Students Forget Up to 60 Percent of Material They Learned in High School," last modified June 25, 2014, universityherald.com/articles/10125/20140625/first-year-college-students-forget-up-to-60-percent-of-material-they-learned-high-school.htm.

2 Naomi O'Brien and LaNesha Tabb, *Unpack Your Impact: How Two Primary Teachers Ditched Problematic Lessons and Built a Culture-Centered Curriculum* (San Diego, CA: Dave Burgess Consulting, Inc., 2020).

3 Ulcca Joshi Hansen, "Why Does Memorization Reign Supreme in Traditional Learning?" Education Reimagined, last modified May 9, 2018, education-reimagined.org/why-memorization-traditional-learning.

4 "Frequently Asked Questions," The Goals Project, goalsproject.org/faqs.html.

5 Rylie Friar, "Kids These Days," filmed April 2019 in El Cajon, CA, TED video, 4:00, youtube.com/watch?v=AZ5jeSOAGh4&list=PLqayKwJOSYYSBcxSD9HH4dy52jgwRvTHv&index=12.

6 Morganne Mallon, "Teenager Starts Volunteer Project to Promote Childhood Literacy," last modified August 6, 2019, pointsoflight.org/awards/teenager-starts-volunteer-project-to-promote-childhood-literacy.

7 Real World Scholars, "The Yearbook '19–'20," docs.google.com/presentation/d/1QlyrfRTUyBX7jKPTHkvHRz2GUfzLYXMi85BMWxWm0jg/edit#slide=id.g9cc88846d2_0_218.

8 "The Future of Jobs Report 2020," World Economic Forum, last modified October 18, 2020, weforum.org/reports/the-future-of-jobs-report-2020.

9 Center for Advanced Professional Studies (CAPS), bvcaps.yourcapsnetwork.org.

10 Ron Berger, Leah Rugen, and Libby Woodfin, *Leaders of Their Own Learning: Transforming Schools Through Student-Engaged Assessment* (San Francisco, CA: Jossey-Bass, 2013).

11 Kristyn Kamps, "Promoting a PBL Mindset: The 'Dimmer Switch' Approach," last modified January 27, 2021, pblworks.org/blog/promoting-pbl-mindset-dimmer-switch-approach.

CHAPTER 10

1 A.J. Juliani, ajjuliani.com.

2 Mary Davenport, "Rethinking Homework This Year—and Beyond," last modified December 16, 2020, edutopia.org/article/rethinking-homework-year-and-beyond?utm_medium=Email&utm_source=ExactTarget&utm_campaign=20201227_News_MindShift_Newsletter&mc_key=00Qi000001ceuWdEAI.

CHAPTER 11

1 Shunryū Suzuki, *Zen Mind, Beginner's Mind: Informal Talks on Zen Meditation and Practice* (Boulder, CO: Shambhala Publications, 2011).

2 "Obedience," Lexico, lexico.com/definition/Obedience.

3 William Bridges, *Managing Transitions: Making the Most of Change* (Philadelphia: Da Capo Press, 1991).

4 Justin Minkel, "Finding the Courage to Teach Past the Fear of 'Getting In Trouble,'" last modified April 4, 2017, edweek.org/education/opinion-finding-the-courage-to-teach-past-the-fear-of-getting-in-trouble/2017/04.

CHAPTER 12

1 Abby Wambach, *Wolfpack: How to Come Together, Unleash Our Power, and Change the Game* (New York: Celadon Books, 2019).

2 Melinda French Gates, *The Moment of Lift: How Empowering Women Changes the World* (New York: Flatiron Books, 2019).

3 Simon Sinek, "How Great Leaders Inspire Action," Ted talk, ted.com/talks/simon_sinek_how_great_leaders_inspire_action.

4 George Couros, "10 Essential Characteristics of a 21st Century Educator," georgecouros.ca/blog/archives/6783.

5 Real World Scholars, realworldscholars.org.

6 Jenny Tolan and Melissa Horwitz, "It Takes a Teacher to Engineer the Classroom for Creativity," last modified October 28, 2016, blog.google/outreach-initiatives/education/it-takes-teach-engineer-classroom-creativity.

7 David Whyte, *Crossing the Unknown Sea: Work as a Pilgrimage of Identity* (New York: Riverhead Books, 2002).

8 Jim Collins, *Good to Great: Why Some Companies Make the Leap and Others Don't* (New York: HarperBusiness, 2001).

9 TEDBlog, "Vulnerability is the Birthplace of Innovation, Creation, and Change: Brené Brown at TED2012," March 2, 2012, https://blog.ted.com/vulnerability-is-the-birthplace-of-innovation-creativity-and-change-brene-brown-at-ted2012.

ACKNOWLEDGMENTS

ABBY AND ZACK: You have made me a better person, teacher, and leader. I am so lucky to be your mom. I learn so much from you both every day, and I hope you know how loved you are, always. May you continue to explore the world, find your passions, hone your talents, and share them with the world. I can't wait to see what the future holds for you both.

MOM AND DAD: There aren't enough words to describe how grateful I am for you two. You have supported me and loved me through it all. I admire you both and couldn't imagine better parents in this world. Thanks for your support and all the "Zoom school" days you took on for the kids so I could write. I appreciate your feedback and conversations that have helped influence my thinking and shaped how I communicate my ideas in this book. I love you!

BILL AND MAR: Thank you for raising the man of my dreams! I am grateful for all you have taught him and continue to teach me and the kids. I am grateful to have your love and support.

GEORGE: You push me, encourage me, and always have my back. Without you, I would be drowning in sticky notes, waiting to figure out the perfect way to say something. Your guidance and nagging reminders have led to opportunities and new ways of thinking that I never imagined were possible. You have a gift for maximizing the talents of others, and I am grateful for all you have done to support me and so many other educators.

DEVIN: I feel so grateful to get to do the work we do, and I am grateful for your perspective, leadership, and future-oriented thinking. Your insights are woven throughout this book, and you have been instrumental in so many of my ideas and practices. Thank you for your thoughtful feedback throughout this process!

TO THE AMAZING EDUCATORS I GET TO WORK WITH, thank you is not nearly enough. I am in awe of the work you do to create amazing learning experiences for your communities, and I am honored to be part of your journey and learn with and from you.

TO MY COLLEAGUES AT LEARNER-CENTERED COLLABORATIVE, you are the best team ever! Each and every one of you at LCC continues to sharpen my thinking and practice. With each interaction, I continue to be inspired by your commitment to supporting the shift to the learner-centered paradigm. Our work is embedded throughout this book and is shaped by our conversations, practices, and reflections. For that and more, I am eternally grateful to get to work with you, and I look forward to what the future holds.

TO THE IMPRESS AND DBC, INC. TEAM, without you, this book would not exist. Thank you for your commitment to sharing the stories of educators and the way you continue to elevate and empower educators. I love being part of the community and am always grateful for your support!

TO THE READING LIST TEAM: Thank you, Sara, for bringing clarity and focus to my ideas, and Lindsey for your guidance through the process. You are truly an amazing team, and I am grateful for how you have helped shape this book!

ABOUT THE AUTHOR

DR. KATIE MARTIN is the chief impact officer at the Learner-Centered Collaborative and author of *Learner-Centered Innovation* and *Evolving Education*. Katie has worked in diverse contexts to learn, research, and support deeper learning for all students. She has served as a middle school English language arts teacher and instructional coach and has led her district's new teacher mentoring program. She teaches in the Graduate School of Education at High Tech High and is on the board of Real World Scholars.

As a leader, educator, and changemaker, Katie's experience in research and practice guides her belief that if we want to change how students learn, we must change how educators learn. She aspires to do that by creating experiences that empower all learners to develop knowledge, skills, and mindsets to thrive in a changing world. As a mom, she wants her kids to have learning experiences in school that build on their strengths and interests, and she is passionate about making sure educators are equipped to do that for all kids.

Connect with Katie:

KatieLMartin.com
Social Media: @KatieMartinEdu

KATIE MARTIN is an engaging speaker and workshop facilitator who customizes learning experiences for your specific context. Katie's heartfelt perspective as a mom and her experience as an educator working with leading schools and districts have shaped her view of not only why we must change how we learn in school but how we can create a culture where learning and innovation are the norm. Katie's mix of research, personal stories, and practical examples will challenge you and your team to create learning experiences that develop the type of learners, workers, and citizens who will thrive in our changing world. Her workshops will inspire you to think about what isn't working, consider what is possible, and lead change in your classroom, school, or district.

Popular Topics from Katie Martin:

- Learning, Teaching, and Leading in a Changing World
- Learner-Centered Innovation
- The Evolving Role of the Educator
- Creating Experiences That Spark Curiosity, Ignite Passion, and Unleash Genius
- Creating a Strengths-Based Culture
- Leveraging Technology to Create Learner-Centered Experiences

To book Dr. Katie Martin to speak at your event, visit KatieLMartin.com.

MORE FROM

ImpressBooks.org

Empower
What Happens when Students Own Their Learning
by A.J. Juliani and John Spencer

Learner-Centered Innovation
Spark Curiosity, Ignite Passion, and Unleash Genius
by Katie Martin

Unleash Talent
Bringing Out the Best in Yourself and the Learners You Serve
by Kara Knollmeyer

Reclaiming Our Calling
Hold On to the Heart, Mind, and Hope of Education
by Brad Gustafson

Take the L.E.A.P.
Ignite a Culture of Innovation
by Elisabeth Bostwick

Drawn to Teach
An Illustrated Guide to Transforming Your Teaching
written by Josh Stumpenhorst and illustrated by Trevor Guthke

Math Recess
Playful Learning in an Age of Disruption
by Sunil Singh and Dr. Christopher Brownell

Innovate inside the Box
Empowering Learners Through UDL and Innovator's Mindset
by George Couros and Katie Novak

Personal & Authentic
Designing Learning Experiences That Last a Lifetime
by Thomas C. Murray

Learner-Centered Leadership
A Blueprint for Transformational Change in Learning Communities
by Devin Vodicka

Kids These Days
A Game Plan for (Re)Connecting with Those We Teach, Lead, & Love
by Dr. Jody Carrington

UDL and Blended Learning
Thriving in Flexible Learning Landscapes
by Katie Novak and Catlin Tucker

Teachers These Days
Stories & Strategies for Reconnection
by Dr. Jody Carrington and Laurie McIntosh

Because of a Teacher
Stories of the Past to Inspire the Future of Education
written and curated by George Couros

Printed in Great Britain
by Amazon

75905306R00122